Understanding Wo

The End of Blame

The Rise of Responsibility

The Return of Feminine Truth

For the woman who wants to feel whole. For the man who wants to understand her. For the daughters yet to be born who deserve to feel safe in their skin.

Heather Ogilvie

Understanding Women

ISBN 978-1-7394347-6-2

Publisher information: Ogilvie Advisory Ltd T/A The Islay Wellness Academy

Disclaimer: This book is intended for informational and inspirational purposes only. It does not constitute medical, psychological, or professional health advice. Always consult with a qualified healthcare provider before making changes to your health or well-being practices.

Understanding Women

Contents

Contents

Understanding Women

Understanding Women

Introduction

For the woman who wants to feel whole. For the man who wants to understand her. For the daughters yet to be born who deserve to feel safe in their skin.

You may not remember exactly when it started — that quiet ache, the push to perform, the sense that being a woman in this world somehow required abandoning something essential. Maybe it began in childhood, where you learned to be pleasing instead of powerful. Maybe it was at school, where logic was rewarded but your deep sensitivity wasn't understood. Maybe it came later, through heartbreak, through burnout, through the slow erosion of your truth while trying to meet everyone else's expectations.

Or maybe it never began at all — because the disconnect has always been there.

This book is a return.
Not to the version of you the world asked you to become — but to the version of you that never stopped whispering beneath it all.

This is not about the "divine feminine" in its over-glossed, misunderstood form.
This is about the true feminine — the energy within you that feels, creates, receives, holds, heals, and flows.
The part of you that was never broken, just buried beneath conditioning.

Understanding Women is a mirror.
It is a reckoning.
It is a return to the truth that feminine energy — inside all of us, regardless of gender — has been distorted, suppressed, and shamed for far too long.

This is a book for the woman who is ready to stop blaming the world and start reclaiming herself.
It's for the woman who lashes out because she's exhausted, who numbs because she's never felt safe enough to feel, who longs to be loved but doesn't know how to receive it.

Understanding Women

It's for the woman who is strong but starving.
Capable, but collapsing.
Powerful, but disconnected from her body, her soul, and her softness.

It's also for the men who want to understand — not control, rescue, or fix — but truly understand the women in their lives. And perhaps more deeply, to understand the feminine inside themselves.

This book does not shame.
It does not divide.
It does not dress up the wounds in spiritual language and call that healing.

It calls things what they are.
It names the aggression in women that no one wants to talk about.
It confronts the self-abandonment we justify as strength.
It dismantles the performative patterns we confuse with empowerment.
It speaks to the epidemic of low self-worth that passes from mother to daughter, from woman to woman, unspoken but deeply felt.

We look honestly at the energies we've inherited:
The distorted masculine that drives without feeling.
The distorted feminine that manipulates, collapses, or controls.
We explore how those energies live within us — not just around us.

We name the five fears that govern the ego — death, illness, rejection, shame, and loss of freedom — and we meet the soul's deepest longing: to be itself, fully, without apology.

We explore boundaries not as walls, but as wise masculine structures that allow the feminine to finally relax and thrive.

We reawaken the intelligence of the body, the Clair senses, the subtle energy field. We reconnect to the nervous system as a guide, the emotions as truth, and the body as a living map.

This is a book about truth.
About integration.

Understanding Women

About growing up the feminine — so she stops needing to be rescued, seen, or saved, and starts becoming the leader, the listener, the lighthouse she was born to be.

It is about women finding themselves.
Men learning how to truly listen.
And a world in which our daughters — those born and yet to be born — can finally feel safe in their own skin.

It speaks of tenderness as sacred.
It speaks of emotional aggression as real.
It speaks of responsibility, not blame — of remembering that no one else is accountable for our inner world but us.

It holds the mirror.
It offers the map.
And it stands as a lighthouse for the woman ready to rise not with force, but with presence.

Because the cage door is open.
But stepping through it will always require a conscious choice.

You are here.
You are ready.
We begin now.

Part One: The Lost Feminine

Understanding Women

Chapter 1: The Masculine Mask We've Been Forced to Wear

"We weren't born to perform. We were born to feel, to create, to trust our own rhythm. But somewhere along the way, we were trained to wear a mask. It's time to remember who we were before the world told us who to be."

— **Heather**

Early Conditioning into Action and Logic

From the moment a girl enters the world, she is observed. Measured. Categorised. Praised for being quiet, calm, and pretty — or corrected if she's loud, messy, or too much. What she learns early on is this: approval is conditional. And very often, what's most rewarded is not her creativity, softness, or sensitivity — but her ability to perform, to behave, and to succeed in systems built for logic and control.

This is where the mask begins.

Conditioning starts quietly. We're praised for getting things right. We're encouraged to compete, achieve, organise, and be responsible. We learn to operate in linear structures and time-bound tasks. The rhythm of the school bell replaces the rhythm of our bodies. Our creative flow becomes secondary to memorisation and measurable outcomes. Intuition is traded for analysis. Sensitivity is framed as weakness. Being emotional is something to be fixed or hidden.

By the time we are teenagers, most of us have already internalised that the world does not make room for the full spectrum of the feminine. We are expected to choose — either suppress our depth to succeed, or be seen as fragile, dramatic, or unstable. For many women, the safest route becomes assimilation into the masculine. Action over rest. Logic over feeling. Doing over being.

And in this subtle switch, something precious is lost.

What we lose is not just the softness or the stillness — it's the deep intelligence of feminine energy. The ability to sense, to feel, to listen within. The connection to cycles, seasons, and the body's wisdom. The intuitive knowing that isn't taught in textbooks but lives in the bones. It's here that we begin living outside of ourselves, evaluating our worth by what we produce or how well we meet expectations, rather than by how deeply we are in tune with our own truth.

The mask of masculine energy isn't inherently wrong. Structure, logic, and action have their sacred place. But when they become our default identity — worn like armour from childhood — we become fragmented. Our true feminine self, the part of us that flows and feels and simply *is*, gets pushed into the shadows.

This chapter is not about blaming the masculine. It's about recognising the conditioning that taught us to disconnect from the truth of who we are. And the first step to remembering is noticing:

- When did you start performing?
- When did your softness get sidelined?
- When did doing become more important than being?

Because the cage door is open.
And the choice to step through it begins here.

How the Feminine Was Suppressed in Childhood and Education

From the very first days of learning — whether at home, nursery, or school — most girls are not taught to trust their inner world. Instead, they are taught to adapt to the outer one.

Understanding Women

We are trained to sit still, follow rules, speak when spoken to, and give the "right" answers. We are graded, marked, and evaluated on our ability to comply, memorise, and perform. Our intelligence is measured in exams and numbers, not in intuition or imagination. Creativity becomes a reward for finishing the "real" work. Sensitivity becomes a problem to manage. And the capacity to feel deeply? That gets labelled as drama, distraction, or disorder.

Somewhere in the process, the connection to our inner world begins to fray.

Education systems, by their very structure, favour left-brain learning: logic, analysis, categorisation, competition. These are qualities associated with masculine energy — not male, but masculine in their function. They are not wrong or harmful in themselves. But when feminine energy — right-brain qualities like emotional processing, creativity, collaboration, receptivity, and empathy — is undervalued, children raised in feminine bodies quickly learn their natural instincts are not the path to success.

So what do we do? We adapt. We shift. We mask.

We become good girls who try harder, stay quiet, suppress big feelings, and smile when we're struggling. We learn to take pride in our ability to push through tiredness, detach from our bodies, and fit into environments that don't allow for ebb and flow. Even in adolescence — when we need space to feel, change, express, and soften — our educational settings become stricter, more pressurised, more focused on outcomes.

By the time we reach adulthood, many of us don't even know how to access our feminine energy anymore. We've been so well trained to function in masculine systems that flow feels unfamiliar, rest feels like failure, and intuition feels irrational. We no longer trust the part of us that feels before it thinks, senses before it speaks, and knows without evidence.

The truth is: our systems do not support the emergence of the feminine. And so the feminine, in most women, becomes stifled — not by nature, but by nurture — or perhaps better phrased as lack of nurture.

Understanding Women

But just because it was conditioned out of us does not mean it is lost. It means we have to *consciously choose* to reconnect. To value feeling as much as thinking. To return to the body. To return to what's natural. To reclaim what was never truly gone — only buried.

Why Feminine Flow Feels Foreign to Modern Women

For many modern women, the idea of *flow* feels not only foreign — it feels unsafe.

We say we want ease, freedom, creativity, rest.
But when space opens up, we rush to fill it.
When emotion rises, we analyse it.
When intuition whispers, we override it with logic.
When we're tired, we push through.
When we ache, we apologise.
When we feel joy, we dim it in case it's "too much."

Why?

Because somewhere along the way, we were taught that *flow is not productive*, that *ease is not earned*, and that *receiving is weak*. We were conditioned to believe that value comes only through output, achievement, and effort. Feminine flow — by its very nature — is nonlinear, non-logical, cyclical. It doesn't follow a to-do list. It doesn't tick boxes. It doesn't compete or rush. It *receives*, it *listens*, it *responds*, it creates. And because of that, it has been labelled inconvenient, unreliable, even dangerous.

Many women have spent years, even decades, running in a direction that denies their nature — until their bodies, hearts, or spirits begin to break down. Burnout. Anxiety. Emotional shutdown. Hormonal imbalance. Creative block. Chronic fatigue. Aggressive Outbursts. All of these are symptoms of a quiet ache that says, "*I can't live like this anymore.*"

We weren't meant to live like this!

Understanding Women

Flow feels foreign not because it isn't ours, but because we've been taught to fear what can't be measured.
To mistrust what can't be proven.
To dismiss what can't be controlled.

But flow is not chaos. Flow is coherence.
It is the deepest intelligence of the feminine.
It is how oceans move. How seeds grow. How love expands. How life breathes.

When women begin to reclaim their flow, something ancient stirs. The body remembers. The mind resists. The soul exhales.

And yes, at first it may feel clumsy. It may feel indulgent or lazy or terrifying. But that's only because we've been living so long in opposition to our essence. We have built empires on exhaustion. We have celebrated stress. We have confused burnout with purpose.

And so when we are invited to soften, to feel, to flow — we freeze.
We say, "*I don't know how.*"
And that is the most honest starting point of all.

The Impact of Over-Masculinisation on Emotional Balance

When a woman spends too long wearing the masculine mask, her emotional world begins to distort. Not because she is broken — but because she has been misaligned for too long.

Masculine energy, when used healthily, offers structure, containment, clarity, and direction. But when overused or unbalanced, it can become rigid, reactive, controlling, and emotionally detached. For a woman, living in this energy too often and for too long creates emotional disconnection — not just from others, but from herself.

She may feel angry and not know why.
Numb, but unable to rest.
Highly capable, but strangely unsatisfied.

Understanding Women

She may keep achieving, performing, producing, yet wonder why joy never really lands. She may feel like she's doing everything "right," but inside, something is missing.

That missing something is *emotional coherence* — the deep alignment between what she feels, what she knows, and how she lives. When feminine energy is suppressed, women lose the capacity to process emotions as they arise. Instead of flowing through her mind and body naturally, her emotions back up. They get stored, swallowed, redirected. They emerge in outbursts, breakdowns, withdrawal, resentment, jealousy, chronic pain, uncontrolled weight gain, excessive weight loss, numbing, addictions, obsessions, or self-sabotage.

Without emotional fluidity, we become emotionally flooded.
Without softness, we become brittle.
Without expression, we implode.

And then, we blame ourselves.
We call it overreacting. We say we're "too sensitive." We try to fix it with more doing, more control, more productivity.
We don't realise that we're trying to solve an energetic imbalance with *the very energy that caused it.*

Over-masculinisation in women doesn't just show up in how we act — it shows up in how we feel, or don't feel.
It affects how we relate to our bodies, our boundaries, our creativity, our partners, our children, and our sense of purpose.

We try to control and correct our imbalance and in doing so create an ever greater imbalance.
And most dangerously of all, it convinces us that this is just the way it is.

But this is not our natural state.
This is not how the feminine was ever meant to live.

It's time to take off the mask.

Understanding Women

Not to discard the masculine within us — but to invite the feminine home.
To return to balance, to emotional truth, and to a way of being that doesn't require us to fight ourselves to feel like we belong.

Because we do belong.
To our bodies.
To our wisdom.
To our feelings.
To ourselves.

Understanding Women

Chapter 2: Why We Can't Thrive in This World

"If you've ever felt like you don't belong here, you're right. You don't belong in a system that demands your suppression. You belong in a world that honours your soul."

— **Heather**

The System Wasn't Built for Us

There's a quiet truth many women carry — but rarely speak: "*This world doesn't work for me.*"

And they're right.
Because it wasn't built for them.

The systems we grow up in — education, work, politics, even medicine — were not designed with the rhythms, needs, and energetic blueprint of the feminine in mind. They were shaped around linear progress, constant output, emotional suppression, and measurable results. These are not inherently wrong values — but they are incomplete. And when they become the only way to succeed, they push entire ways of being to the edges.

For women, this creates a lifelong pressure to adapt rather than to belong.

From an early age, we learn that the safest way to navigate the world is to suppress what is natural in us and amplify what is expected. We are taught to override our body's cues, to mistrust our intuition, and to measure success by what we can prove instead of what we can feel. Productivity is praised. Performance is rewarded. Presence, emotion, and cyclical energy are not just undervalued — they're invisible.

And so, we shrink.

Understanding Women

Not in size, but in soul.

We become less expressive, less curious, less connected to our own instincts. We stop asking, "*Does this feel right?*" and start asking, "*Is this acceptable?*" We start living to be palatable rather than powerful.

This is not just an individual wound — it's systemic.
And it shows up everywhere:

- In schools that punish movement, emotion, creativity, and non-linear thinking.
- In workplaces that reward burnout and punish rest.
- In social systems that dismiss emotional labour while glorifying productivity.
- In families where daughters are raised to be accommodating, quiet, and grateful for less.

When a woman says she's exhausted, she often means: "I am tired of trying to be someone I'm not."
And when a woman says she feels like she's failing, she often means: "I am trying to succeed in a system that was never designed for my wholeness."

This chapter is not about rebellion — it's about realisation.

Because the moment a woman understands that the world wasn't made for her truth, she can stop seeing herself as broken — and begin to rebuild her life around what actually nourishes her.

Creativity, Emotion, and Flow Don't Fit the Rules

If the feminine had a language, it would be creativity.
If it had a compass, it would be emotion.
And if it had a rhythm, it would be flow.

But none of these speak the language of the current system.

Understanding Women

The structures we're asked to succeed within — school curriculums, corporate ladders, even personal development frameworks — are almost entirely built on predictability, consistency, logic, and control. They reward repetition. They prize output. They celebrate what can be tracked, quantified, and rationally explained.

Feminine energy does not move like that.

Creativity cannot be summoned on a schedule. Emotion does not operate in neat, linear patterns. Flow arrives on its own time, through its own portals — often in the spaces between action, in the quiet, in the listening.

So what happens when these natural feminine expressions try to exist inside unnatural environments?

They become distorted. Suppressed. Pathologised.
We call emotion "too much."
We call creativity a "nice-to-have."
We call flow "laziness" or "distraction."

And slowly, without even realising it, women begin to disown the very parts of themselves that were meant to guide them.

We silence our emotional truth in favour of being agreeable.
We hide our creative ideas because they don't fit the mould.
We override our desire to pause because the deadline is more important than the body's need to breathe.

And somewhere deep inside, the feminine whispers: "*This isn't how I was meant to live.*"

But she is not gone. She is waiting.

Waiting to be recognised not as a weakness or indulgence, but as a profound intelligence. Creativity is not a luxury — it's our life force. Emotion is not unstable — it is a sacred signal system. Flow is not a flaw — it's a current of wisdom designed to guide us back to balance.

Understanding Women

We can't thrive in systems that shame what we are made of.

But we can begin to create new ways of being — where creativity leads, emotion is honoured, and flow is trusted as a path, not a problem.

How Performance Culture Punishes Feminine Energy?

Our world is obsessed with results. Performance has become the gold standard of worth. But performance culture doesn't just shape how we work — it shapes how we *exist*.

It tells us:

- You are only as valuable as your output.
- You must prove your worth daily.
- Rest is earned, not inherent.
- Visibility matters more than truth.
- If you slow down, you fall behind.

This might sound like modern motivation — but to the feminine, it's spiritual starvation.

Performance culture is rooted in masculine energy: forward motion, external validation, outcome over process. When this becomes the default measure of success, anything that doesn't conform — emotional processing, deep reflection, creative wandering, embodied intuition — is quietly punished.

Not always by others. Often, by ourselves.

We internalise the pace. We push when we need to pause. We work when we're bleeding, smiling through tears, dismissing signals from the body as inconvenience. We see our cyclical nature as a liability, not a gift.

The result?

Women feel disconnected. Not because they aren't trying hard enough — but because they are living in contradiction to their design.

Understanding Women

The feminine doesn't perform. She expresses. She *emerges*. She *feels*. Her power comes from presence, not perfection. But in a system that only sees what's delivered, not what's embodied, the feminine becomes invisible — and eventually, exhausted.

Performance culture also breeds comparison. In spaces where constant output is the norm, women don't just compete with men — they begin to compete with each other. Who's coping better? Who's producing more? Who's got it together? Behind the scenes, many are burning out, breaking down, or silently screaming, "*This isn't sustainable.*"

And they're right. It's not.

We weren't meant to perform life.
We were meant to live it — sensitively, cyclically, honestly.

When the feminine returns, she doesn't compete. She connects. She doesn't hustle. She harmonises. And she knows: her worth was never meant to be measured in performance.

Her worth has always been in her truthful presence.

The Inner Conflict of Conforming vs. Authenticity

Every woman, at some point, feels the split.

The tension between *who she is expected to be* and *who she truly is.*
The pressure to meet the moment — and the longing to be met, just as she is.
The desire to succeed — and the craving to simply be at peace.

This inner conflict runs deep, because the world has rewarded us for conforming while our souls have been quietly aching for truth.

Authenticity isn't just about "being yourself" — it's about *reclaiming the parts of you that were never allowed to exist fully.* It's about remembering what you needed to suppress in order to be liked, loved, or accepted. And it's about recognising where those masks still linger: in your voice, your choices, your posture, your silence.

Understanding Women

Conforming feels safe — until it starts to erode your centre.

And authenticity feels risky — until you realise it's the only place that feels like home.

Women are intuitive by nature, and we know when we're out of alignment. But we also know the cost of rocking the boat. So we stay quiet when we want to speak. We smile when we want to scream. We stay when our soul wants to go. And we call it loyalty, or kindness, or patience — but often, it's just fear. Fear of losing love. Fear of being too much. Fear of not being enough.

This conflict — between external conformity and internal truth — is exhausting. And the longer we live with it, the more disconnected we become.

From our bodies.
From our voices.
From our joy.
From each other.

But here's the turning point: the moment we start to value our authenticity more than our approval, the game changes. The inner conflict quiets. The energy spent performing returns to presence. And the choices that once felt impossible begin to feel inevitable.

Because the truth is: the woman you really are is already whole.
She doesn't need to be improved. She needs to be *allowed*.

Understanding Women

Chapter 3: The Energetic Imbalance Inside Every Woman

"Every person holds both masculine and feminine energy — but we were never taught how to let them dance. We were taught to choose one, wear it like armour, and lose ourselves through imbalance."

— Heather

Understanding Feminine and Masculine Energies Within

Every human being carries both masculine and feminine energy. This is not about gender — it's about *energetic design*. And yet, most of us have been raised to reject, misunderstand, or over-identify with one side while disowning the other.

Feminine energy is the energy of flow.
Masculine energy is the energy of form.
Feminine feels. Masculine focuses.
Feminine opens. Masculine protects.
Feminine expresses. Masculine holds.

In an ideal world, these two energies move together like breath — inhalation and exhalation, ebb and flow, giving and receiving. But in reality, most people — especially women — are energetically imbalanced. And they don't even know it.

For women, this imbalance often looks like living in a constant state of doing, organising, managing, planning, controlling. Even when rest is possible, they can't relax. Even when help is offered, they can't receive it. Because their internal masculine is overdeveloped, while their feminine is undernourished. The result? Exhaustion. Disconnection. Emotional repression. An inability to soften — even when the soul is screaming for it.

Understanding Women

For men, the imbalance often looks different. Many men have been taught that their masculinity is only valid when it's dominant, stoic, or emotionally detached. Their feminine energy — their sensitivity, their intuition, their empathy — is often buried beneath shame or ridicule. They may struggle to express vulnerability or process emotion because the feminine within them has been deemed unacceptable.

The distortion lives on both sides.
And so does the healing.

Masculine energy in its purest form is protective, clear, grounded, and honourable. Feminine energy in its purest form is intuitive, nurturing, expressive, and creative.

Both are sacred. Both are needed.
And both are wildly misunderstood.

Inside of women, these energies are meant to dance. The feminine leads from within — the centre of feeling, sensing, and truth. The masculine surrounds it with strength, direction, and boundaries. But when this relationship is reversed — when the masculine takes over the centre — we become disconnected from our emotional body and start running life like a checklist instead of a sacred rhythm.

Inside of men, the dance is different — but just as vital. Masculine essence may lead, but without a healthy inner feminine, a man becomes hardened, ungrounded, and relationally unavailable. His intuition dulls. His presence fades. His capacity for empathy shrinks.

Understanding this balance is not about becoming half-and-half. It's about returning to your *natural energetic essence* — and allowing the other energy to serve and support that essence.

This isn't theory. It's how we live, how we love, how we lead, and how we heal.

Understanding Women

The Rise of the Distorted Feminine and Masculine

When we speak about *distorted energy*, we're not talking about evil or brokenness — we're talking about energy that has been misused, misunderstood, or shaped by trauma, conditioning, or fear.

Masculine and feminine energies, in their purest form, are beautiful forces of nature. But when they become distorted — within women or within men — they create confusion, pain, and disconnection.

Let's start by looking at each in their essence.

True Masculine Energy is:

- Grounded
- Protective (not controlling)
- Clear and direct
- Responsible and accountable
- Focused and dependable
- Creates structure and stability

It holds. It builds. It provides containment so that life can safely expand within it.

True Feminine Energy is:

- Intuitive
- Receptive
- Nurturing
- Creative
- Expressive
- Emotionally intelligent

It flows. It feels. It creates connection, beauty, and meaning.

Understanding Women

Both are powerful. Both are sacred.
But when twisted by fear, trauma, or unhealed patterns, their distortions emerge.

Distorted Masculine Energy becomes:

- Controlling
- Aggressive
- Emotionally shut down
- Dismissive or domineering
- Obsessed with power, achievement, or dominance
- Violent or abusive in thought, word, or action

This is the version of masculinity that tries to lead without listening. It overpowers rather than protects. It suppresses feeling, intuition, and vulnerability, seeing them as threats. In both men and women, distorted masculine energy creates a sense of hyper-independence, disconnection from the body, and a deep fear of "losing control."

Distorted Feminine Energy becomes:

- Manipulative
- Victimised
- Emotionally volatile
- Passive-aggressive
- Over-sacrificing or self-abandoning
- Unable to set or hold boundaries

This is the version of femininity that feels unsafe and ungrounded. It expresses emotion but doesn't process it. It clings rather than connects. It loses itself in others and resents them for it. In both women and men, distorted feminine energy shows up as moodiness, martyrdom, or emotional chaos — often hiding deep wounds of not being seen, heard, or protected.

Understanding Women

Every one of us carries some version of these distortions, because we've all been shaped by systems and relationships that did not know how to honour or model healthy energy dynamics.

Women who grew up without strong, safe, present role models often overdevelop their inner masculine to protect themselves. They become hyper-independent, emotionally armoured, and overly responsible. At the same time, if they didn't see the feminine being honoured, they may carry shame about softness, emotionality, or rest — and suppress it until it bursts out sideways.

Men, similarly, may suppress their own softness and live from a hardened version of masculinity that cuts them off from empathy and intuition — or they may over-identify with their inner feminine, losing their ability to hold direction and lead with grounded presence.

This isn't about gender roles — it's about *energetic health*.
Healing begins with recognising the imbalance, naming the distortions, and remembering this:

The true feminine is not weak. The true masculine is not cruel.

Both are needed. And when they are restored to right relationship — within ourselves and with each other — balance returns.

Why Balance is Not 50/50 – It's Rooted in Essence

One of the most common misconceptions around masculine and feminine energy is the idea that balance means splitting them evenly — 50% masculine, 50% feminine. But this is not how true energetic harmony works.

Balance is not about sameness. It's about *alignment with your true inner essence*.

Every person — regardless of gender — has a core energetic essence. For some, that essence is naturally more feminine. For others, it is more masculine. The key to balance isn't blending the two equally — it's *centering your life around the one that is true to your core, while allowing the other to support and protect it.*

A feminine-essence person (most women) will feel balanced when:

- Their inner feminine leads with intuition, creativity, and emotional truth
- Their inner masculine provides structure, safety, and protection without dominating
- They feel free to express, connect, and flow without fear of judgment
- They trust their body, their rhythms, and their cycles

In this setup, feminine energy holds the centre. It is the core expression. Masculine energy is the *container*. It sets boundaries, makes decisions when needed, and helps take action in alignment with the feminine's truth.

A masculine-essence person (most men) will feel balanced when:

- Their inner masculine leads with purpose, focus, and grounded clarity
- Their inner feminine offers sensitivity, openness, and emotional intelligence
- They feel free to take action without cutting off from their heart
- They trust their gut, their instincts, and their capacity to hold space

In this case, the masculine is the centre, and the feminine softens and opens the way to deeper wisdom, empathy, and relational depth.

The problem arises when we try to override our essence.
When a feminine-essence woman lives from her masculine all day, every day, she feels depleted, tight, disconnected, and eventually resentful.
When a masculine-essence man is never allowed to express direction, clarity, or instinctive knowing, he feels lost, uncertain, and disempowered.

This is why the 50/50 ideal often fails. It assumes sameness where there is difference. It ignores the deeper energetic blueprint that lives in each soul.

And perhaps most importantly: it places balance outside of the body, as an intellectual idea, instead of inside the body, as an *embodied truth.*

Energetic balance is deeply personal. It comes from listening within — not just to what the world tells you is "balanced," but to what your soul *feels* like when it's not split, not striving, not compensating — just being exactly what it is.

That is the balance we are returning to.

Ceremonially Reclaiming Feminine Centre, Masculine Perimeter

If you've lived your whole life with your inner masculine in the driver's seat, softening back into your true feminine centre may feel unfamiliar — even frightening.

But it isn't about becoming someone else. It's about *returning to who you were before you learned to lead with armour instead of essence.*

The feminine belongs in the centre.
She is the pulse, the warmth, the wisdom that moves from within.
She senses what is true. She feels what is unseen. She creates, she expresses, she *is.*
When the feminine leads from the centre, we feel whole — because we are living from our truth.

The masculine belongs at the perimeter.
Not to dominate or control — but to protect.
He is the container, the boundary, the clear line between what serves and what doesn't.
When the masculine stands guard around the feminine — not over her — he gives her the freedom to feel safe enough to soften.

Most of us have reversed this.
We've placed the masculine at the core — logic, control, performance — and buried the feminine beneath layers of survival.
Reclaiming the feminine centre is an act of restoration.
It's also a profound ceremony of choice.

Here's one way to begin:

- Close your eyes.
- Visualise your body.
- Visualise your energy.

Where is your feminine? Is she present? Is she hiding? Does she feel safe?

Now gently ask your masculine energy to step back — not away, but back — toward the perimeter. Ask him to become your protector, not your ruler. Ask him to set boundaries, to hold space, to keep you safe — but not to silence your truth.

Then invite your feminine to rise, slowly, gently.
Let her take up space at the centre.
Let her guide you with feeling, not force.
Let her remind you that you are not here to push — you are here to be.

This isn't a one-time ritual. It's a lifelong rebalancing.

But every time you make that choice — every time you say *no* to pushing, yes to listening, *no* to proving, yes to presence — you move back into right relationship with yourself.

You come home.

And once you are home in your body, your truth, your energy — everything else begins to rearrange itself around that centre.
Relationships shift. Emotions settle. Creativity returns. Peace becomes possible.

This is the return to balance.
Not balance as equality.
But balance as harmony.
Balance as truth.

Part Two: The Mirror of Modern Womanhood

Understanding Women

Chapter 4: Jealousy, Judgment, and Internalised Aggression

"Emotional aggression is still aggression. And until we stop dressing our wounds in spiritual language, we'll keep wounding ourselves and others in the name of healing."

— ***Heather***

How Unmet Emotional Needs Become Weapons

There's a shadow side of modern womanhood that too many women don't want to look at — but it's time. Because what we refuse to face, we keep repeating. And what we keep repeating, we end up becoming.

Here is the truth: unmet emotional needs do not disappear. They mutate.

If a woman does not feel seen, heard, valued, safe, or loved — those unmet needs don't vanish.
They twist. They tighten. They spill out sideways. And too often, they land on other women.

What should have been expressed becomes projected.
What should have been felt becomes weaponised.
What should have been healed becomes a cycle of hurt disguised as power.

Women begin stalking each other on social media — not just out of curiosity, but from obsession, insecurity, jealousy. Noticing every detail of someone else's life, body, relationship, success — not to celebrate it, but to compare, diminish, or judge.

A woman might not be angry at her friend. She might be angry at life.

Understanding Women

But the unmet need within her is so loud, it finds the nearest outlet — and sometimes that's the person she was supposed to love, support, or stand beside.

This is how bitchiness is born. This is how passive-aggression becomes culture. This is how judgment turns from a protective mechanism into a weapon.

And it isn't because women are inherently cruel — it's because they are disconnected from their own needs.
They haven't been taught how to identify, express, and tend to what they're really feeling.
So instead, those feelings become ammunition.

- If I feel unworthy, I'll make you feel small.
- If I feel left behind, I'll attack your success
- If I feel invisible, I'll make sure someone else is seen *less*.
- If I don't know how to say "*I'm hurting*," I'll lash out instead.

The saddest part?
This aggression doesn't make us feel better.
It doesn't make us feel bigger.
It doesn't make us feel powerful.

It leaves us more hollow. More ashamed. More alone.

Because the truth is: when we attack another woman, we are often attacking the part of ourselves we have not yet dared to love.

The antidote isn't pretending to be nice. It's not bypassing the rage.
It's getting real. Getting honest. Owning the unmet need. Naming the pain underneath the pattern. And choosing a different way.

Because until we do, we're not just hurting each other. We're destroying our own evolution.

Understanding Women

The Trap of Comparison Without Growth

Comparison has become a reflex activity — especially among women.
But what's often called "comparison" is actually a much deeper issue: *self-abandonment in disguise.*

We scroll through images of other women's lives — bodies, relationships, successes, styles — not to be inspired, but to find evidence that we're not enough.
And when we feel that internal sting of inadequacy, we rarely pause to ask *why.* Instead, we judge.

Her success? Must be fake.
Her relationship? Probably performative.
Her joy? It won't last.
Her beauty? Edited, filtered, bought.

We don't realise that what we're criticising is the exact thing we're yearning for.
And because we haven't been taught how to honour longing as sacred — we weaponise it instead.

This is the trap: when comparison lacks growth, it becomes destruction.

Not just of other women — but of ourselves.

It chips away at our capacity to celebrate, to connect, to collaborate. It replaces genuine admiration with internalized scarcity. It creates a culture where no one is allowed to shine without someone trying to dim the light. And beneath all of it is one core wound: *I don't feel like I'm enough as I am.*

Here's the hard truth: emotional aggression is violence.
It may not bruise skin, but it bruises souls.
It erodes trust. It fractures relationships. It shuts down softness.
It builds walls between women who were meant to support each other.

Understanding Women

Aggression doesn't only look like shouting or insulting — it also looks like constant correction, the need to be seen as the smartest, the most moral, the most right in every room. It looks like dismissing another woman's experience because it threatens your own. It looks like hiding criticism in jokes, or masking control as "helpfulness."

This behaviour doesn't make you right. It makes you disconnected.

And it doesn't come from power. It comes from pain.

Comparison without growth, jealousy without awareness, judgment without ownership — these are acts of self-harm projected outward.
They don't elevate us. They empty us.

The way forward isn't to shut down comparison — it's to *listen to it.*
"What does this reaction show me about what I desire?"
"Where do I still feel not enough?"
"And how can I grow into the woman who celebrates instead of competes?"

Reclaiming Sisterhood Without Pretending

There's a deep ache in women today. An ache for connection.
We want real sisterhood.
We want spaces where we can be soft, expressive, seen, and held.

But too often, those spaces become battlegrounds.
Not overtly — but energetically.
Small jabs, unspoken comparison, subtle withdrawal, power plays in disguise.

Women's circles, friendships, collaborations — they carry such potential. But they also carry the residue of lifetimes of suppression, betrayal, and internalised fear. Many women still don't feel safe in the presence of other women. And the hard part is — they have good reason.

Because we've been taught to see each other as competition.

Understanding Women

Because we've been hurt by other women.
Because we've hurt other women, even if we didn't mean to.
And because so many of us are still walking around with unhealed wounds disguised as personality traits.

So what do we do?

Some try to reclaim sisterhood by pretending — forced positivity, fake support, surface-level affirmation. But pretending isn't healing. It's just more performance.

Reclaiming sisterhood doesn't start with group hugs and affirmations. It starts with *accountability*.

It starts with saying:

- *"I've been jealous before, and I want to understand why."*
- *"I've judged other women for things I haven't allowed myself to feel."*
- *"I've shut people out because I didn't know how to stay soft while feeling triggered."*
- *"I've been the woman who hurt another woman — and I want to change."*

Sisterhood is sacred — but only when it is honest.

You cannot reclaim something you won't tell the truth about. And you cannot build safety in spaces where truth is not allowed to breathe.

So we begin here. With honesty. With women willing to stop pretending they're always kind, always evolved, always supportive. With women willing to *look at themselves* — not just through a spiritual lens, but a very real, grounded one.

Because when you do the work to clean up the energy you bring into sisterhood, you make space for other women to do the same.

Not perfectly. But truthfully.
And that is the soil where something real can grow.

Understanding Women

The Courage to Own Our Shadow Traits

Every woman has a shadow.

That doesn't make you broken. It makes you human.
But here's the part most women don't want to face: if you don't own your shadow, it will own you.

It will hijack your friendships, sabotage your relationships, and make you believe your pain is everyone else's fault. It will twist your unhealed wounds into weapons. And worst of all — it will convince you you're "doing the work" while you're actually just doing the performance.

Let's stop sugarcoating this.

Most women are not doing the real work. They're talking about growth. They're reposting quotes. They're lighting candles and journaling intentions. But the second discomfort shows up — real, raw, mirror-in-the-face discomfort — they turn outward and start pointing fingers.

"He's a narcissist."
"That energy is toxic."
"She's jealous of me."
"That group just isn't aligned anymore."

Sound familiar?

The second someone mirrors something back to us that we haven't owned — we call it a red flag. We ghost. We blame. We exit.

And this is not healing. This is *avoidance*.

You cannot fix your life by judging other people.
You cannot grow by calling everything misaligned and walking away.
And you cannot be at peace while still needing to be seen as right.

Understanding Women

This is deflection.
This is the ego dressing up in spiritual robes and pretending it's self-aware.
This is bypassing the truth that needs to be faced:

Nobody is coming to save you from the parts of yourself you refuse to own.

Let's get brutally honest:

- If you're still calling everyone else toxic, maybe it's your boundaries that are unclear.
- If everyone you date is a narcissist, maybe you're addicted to the pattern of being needed, then abandoned.
- If you're constantly feeling sacrificed, martyred, misused — maybe you're still deriving your identity from suffering.
- If you manipulate, control, punish with silence or sharpness and call it "intuition," it's not. It's fear.

And if that offends you — good.
Because it means the truth is brushing up against the part of you that knows it's time to grow up.

You cannot build a life of peace while carrying a mind full of blame.
You cannot build healthy relationships when you still believe pain is something caused only from the outside.
And you cannot become the woman you're here to be until you stop outsourcing your pain and start reclaiming your power.

The shadow is not the problem.
Your refusal to see it is.

Here's what true self-awareness looks like:

- *"I hurt someone because I was hurt."*
- *"I judged her because I felt insecure."*
- *"I needed to be seen as right because I felt unseen in myself."*

- *"I lashed out because I didn't know how to sit with my shame."*

This is not weakness. This is maturity. It's what separates women who pretend to be empowered from those who *actually* are. You can't keep sacrificing your potential on the altar of your unwillingness to be uncomfortable.

You want real healing?
Then ask yourself:

- "When did I last take full responsibility for the way I showed up in conflict?"
- "When did I last apologise not to be the bigger person — but because I was actually wrong?"
- "When did I last admit, out loud, that I hurt someone else because I didn't know how to soothe my own shame?"

This is what growth looks like. It's not pretty. It's not comfortable. It doesn't come with a crystal or a caption. But it is real.

And until you're willing to go there — to sit with the woman who lashes out, shuts down, belittles, manipulates, or collapses — you'll keep looping through relationships, friendships, careers, and choices that reflect the wounds you've never tended to.

You want to be powerful? Be accountable.
You want to feel peace? Stop needing to be right.
You want to lead others? Learn to lead yourself through your own shadow first.

The women who transform are not perfect.
They are *willing*.
Willing to look.
Willing to feel.
Willing to own what isn't working and shift it from the inside out.

This chapter isn't here to shame you. It's here to wake you up. Because we cannot keep blaming the world for a war we're still waging within. Freedom begins the moment you stop needing to be right, and start choosing to be whole.

Chapter 5. The Rise of the Emotionally Malnourished Woman

"You didn't lose yourself in a relationship, or a job, or motherhood, or your upbringing. You lost yourself in the moment you stopped believing your needs were valid."

— ***Heather***

How We Abandon Ourselves Before Anyone Else Does

Before anyone else walks away, before the world disappoints us, before the relationship fails — we often abandon ourselves first.

We override our inner knowing to keep the peace.
We quiet our needs to avoid seeming needy.
We numb our feelings to stay "in control."
We say yes to things our whole body is screaming no to.
And when it all breaks down later, we wonder why it hurts so much.

It hurts because the very first betrayal wasn't from them.
It was from us.

Most emotionally malnourished women don't realise they are starving — because they've been praised for how well they've learned to function without being fed.

Fed with presence.
Fed with emotional truth.
Fed with real connection, softness, tenderness, safety.

Understanding Women

We are not nourished by food alone.
We are nourished by *feeling met*.
By feeling seen, heard, held, loved, and understood.

And yet, somewhere along the way, most women were taught that these needs were "too much."
That needing to be seen was vanity.
That needing to be loved deeply was weakness.
That needing to be heard made you dramatic.
That needing to rest made you lazy.
So we trained ourselves to stop needing altogether.

But the need didn't go away.
It simply went underground — and started to leak out sideways.
Through over-giving.
Through bitterness.
Through silent resentment.
Through compulsive busyness.
Through emotional collapse and chronic self-abandonment.

This is what creates the emotionally malnourished woman:

- She smiles while starving.
- She shows up for everyone but herself.
- She gives what she doesn't have.
- She rationalises away the ache.
- She wears independence like a badge while quietly longing to be held.

And none of this makes her weak.
It makes her *disconnected*.

Disconnection from self is the root of emotional malnourishment.
Not just disconnection from what we feel, but from what we *need* — and the belief that those needs are valid, safe, and worthy of being met.

Understanding Women

This is not a personality flaw.
This is conditioning.
But just because it's been your pattern doesn't mean it has to be your future.

This chapter is here to help you see where you left yourself behind — and begin calling yourself home.

Self-Sacrifice Disguised as Love

Many women don't recognise their self-sacrifice because it looks so much like love.

They give.
They show up.
They carry.
They make space.
They anticipate needs.
They overextend.
They smile through it all.

And they call it devotion.
They call it care.
They call it being a "good woman," a "supportive partner," a "strong mother," a "loyal friend."

But what they're actually doing is *abandoning themselves in the name of connection.*

This is not love.
This is self-erasure.

True love includes you. It doesn't ask you to disappear, to dim your light, to swallow your words, or to become an empty vessel for someone else's comfort.

But for many women, disappearing is the first thing they learned to do.

Understanding Women

We were taught to be accommodating, to be agreeable, to put others first.
We were praised for being easy to love — not for being deeply ourselves.
So we began equating sacrifice with value.
We believed the more we gave, the more worthy we were.

And over time, we started offering everything — except ourselves.

The emotionally malnourished woman often doesn't know how to receive.
She confuses boundaries with rejection.
She confuses being needed with being loved.
And she ends up in relationships, friendships, and families where she is slowly disappearing — and calling it closeness.

But here's the truth:

Sacrifice without self-respect is not sacred.
It's self-abandonment.
And love that costs you your voice, your peace, or your aliveness is not love — it's bondage.

This chapter isn't asking you to stop loving others.
It's asking you to stop confusing *overgiving* with love.
To stop calling depletion devotion.
To stop offering so much of yourself that there's nothing left for you.

Because you are not more lovable when you are invisible.
You are not more worthy when you are exhausted.
You are not more spiritual when you are silent.

The most powerful love is one that includes you.
And the most radical act of love you can offer the world is to stop abandoning yourself.

Understanding Women

The Shame of Wanting to Be Seen and Loved

Most women won't say it out loud — but deep down, they want to be seen.
They want to be adored.
They want to be known, cherished, chosen.
Not just for what they give, but for who they are when they're not giving anything at all.

But somewhere along the way, that wanting became *shameful.*
And so they buried it.

We are taught to aspire to independence, strength, self-sufficiency.
So needing anything — especially love — starts to feel like a weakness.

We mock ourselves:

- *"I don't need anyone."*
- *"I'm fine on my own."*
- *"I'd rather be alone than disappointed."*

We say we want to be understood, but when love arrives, we don't know how to receive it.
We push it away.
We test it.
We doubt it.
We sabotage it.
Because underneath it all, we're terrified it won't stay.
Or worse — that it never saw us clearly to begin with.

There is a specific kind of grief that lives in a woman who has gone unseen for too long.
She stops expressing.
She stops asking.
She learns to dim her desires because no one ever took them seriously.
She learns to silence her truth because she's tired of not being heard.

Eventually, she starts to believe that maybe love just isn't for her.

But the truth is: *it's not her desire that's the problem — it's the shame that has been wrapped around it.*

There is nothing wrong with wanting to be deeply seen.
To be looked at and understood, felt and witnessed.
To be loved in a way that touches your soul, not just your surface.

There is nothing wrong with needing connection.
What's wrong is that we've been taught to carry that need in silence.

The emotionally malnourished woman doesn't just lack love from others.
She lacks the inner permission to *admit she wants it.*

This is where healing begins.
Not by pretending you don't need anything.
But by standing inside your full humanity and saying:

"Yes, I want to be seen. I want to be loved. And I will not shame myself for this ever again."

Practices for Emotional Re-Nourishment

Emotional malnourishment doesn't heal with theory.
It heals with practice.
With small, daily choices to come back into relationship with yourself — gently, truthfully, and consistently.

Here are some simple but powerful practices to begin re-nourishing the parts of you that have gone unseen, unfelt, and unloved:

Name What You Need

Most women don't feel nourished because they don't know what they need — or they're too ashamed to say it.

Understanding Women

Start by asking yourself, daily:

- *"What do I need right now?"*
- *"What am I feeling, and what would help me hold that feeling with care?"*
- *"What am I craving, emotionally — not just physically or mentally?"*

Write it down. Speak it out loud. Let it exist.
Even if no one else meets that need — you begin by honouring it yourself.

Interrupt the Pattern of Over-Giving

Before you say yes to that favour, that text, that plan, that obligation — pause.

Ask:

- *"Is this a gift or a performance?"*
- *"Am I giving from fullness or from guilt?"*
- *"If I say no, would I still feel like I matter?"*

Start choosing based on truth, not on habit.
Let "no" be a complete sentence when needed.
Let "yes" come from wholeness.

Speak What You've Buried

Find a journal, a voice note app, a safe friend, or a mirror. Say the things you've never let yourself say.

- *"I want to be loved."*
- *"I feel lonely, even when I look like I'm thriving."*
- *"I don't want to hold everything anymore."*

This isn't indulgent.
This is emotional clarity.
The more honestly you speak your feelings, the more space they have to move and heal.

Understanding Women

Reclaim Ritual

Create small daily rituals that feed your feminine nervous system.
This could be five minutes of breathing. A quiet tea. A slow walk. A bath without your phone.
It doesn't have to be big. But it has to be *for you*.

These moments teach your system:
"I am safe to rest. I am allowed to receive. I matter."

Practice Receiving Without Apology

Let someone help you.
Let someone compliment you without deflecting.
Let yourself feel joy without guilt.
Let yourself be held without needing to earn it.

Receiving is not weak. It is the feminine in action.
And every time you receive with openness, you rewrite the belief that says you have to do everything alone.

These practices are not about fixing yourself.
They're about *feeding yourself*.

You don't have to heal everything overnight.
You just have to stop starving your emotional self and start tending to her, moment by moment, with presence and love.

This is how we return.
This is how we re-nourish.
This is how we finally come home to ourselves.

Understanding Women

Chapter 6. The Virus of Low Self-Worth

"You can't build a life you love from a belief that you aren't enough. Worth is not a reward. It's your foundation."

— ***Heather***

How It Spreads Quietly Through Thought and Belief

Low self-worth doesn't usually enter through the front door. It slips in quietly, subtly — through the cracks in our thoughts, the tone of a comment, the shape of a memory, the silence that followed a truth we were too young to hold alone.

It is not always loud.
It doesn't always shout "*You're not good enough.*"
Instead, it whispers:

- "*That was too much.*"
- "*They didn't text back — you probably said something wrong.*"
- "*You should be further ahead by now.*"
- "*She's prettier.*"
- "*You've always been the difficult one.*"

And you don't question it, because you've heard it so many times before. That's how it spreads — through repetition, not reality. Through the unconscious beliefs we've picked up from parents, teachers, friends, media, systems, and social norms that condition us to measure ourselves by something outside of ourselves.

We don't wake up one day and say "*I don't believe I'm enough.*"
It happens slowly.
Thought by thought.

Understanding Women

Comment by comment.
Experience by experience.

Until it becomes a lens we look through.
Not just about one thing — but about *everything*.

And because it's subtle, we don't always recognise it.
We call it "insecurity."
We call it "impostor syndrome."
We call it "just the way I've always been."

But low self-worth is not a personality trait.
It is a virus.
It infects the way we speak, think, act, love, lead, and live.
And like any virus, it adapts. It hides. It thrives in silence and shame.

It affects the woman who doubts herself in every meeting, even though she's qualified.
It affects the woman who over-prepares, over-delivers, over-explains.
It affects the woman who dates men who mirror back her lack of value.
It affects the woman who never rests because she's terrified of feeling unproductive.
It affects the woman who cannot accept a compliment, a helping hand, a moment of praise — without brushing it off or earning it ten times over.

And most of all, it affects the woman who doesn't even know it's there — because she's gotten so good at pretending she's fine.

Low self-worth is not always dramatic.
It's the quietest voice in the room — but it's the one that decides how far we go, how much we allow, how fully we show up.

And unless we start to trace it back to its root — and *name it for what it is* — we'll keep trying to "fix" our lives on the surface, while the core stays untouched.

This chapter is about going to the core.

Understanding Women

Why We Seek Validation Instead of Love

Love is deep. It's rooted. It's whole.
Validation is fleeting. It's addictive. It's empty.

And too often, we confuse the two.

Because when your self-worth is low, love feels too *real.*
Too raw.
Too exposing.
Too dependent on you being seen — not as a role, or a performance, but as you actually are.

And if you don't believe that "you" is enough, love feels dangerous.
So instead, we reach for validation.

Validation gives us short hits of approval without the risk of intimacy.
It's the quick fix for a deeper ache.

- A like.
- A compliment.
- A text back.
- A reaction.
- A look.
- A "well done."
- A "you're so strong."

We chase it, because it's predictable.
It doesn't require us to open our hearts.
It doesn't require us to be vulnerable.
It doesn't require us to *receive.*

But it never fills us. It only feeds the hunger.

Understanding Women

Women have been conditioned to seek validation from the outside because most were never taught to trust what's inside.

We learned to be the good girl. The clever one. The pretty one. The sporty one. The helpful one. The nice one.
We learned to earn our worth through performance.
We learned to shape-shift based on approval.
We learned to edit ourselves before anyone else could.

So, of course, we reach for validation — it's the language we were taught.

Love, on the other hand, speaks a language many of us never learned:
Presence. Honesty. Acceptance. Stillness. Being known.

And that's confronting when you've built an entire identity around being palatable rather than present.

Validation keeps us in a loop.
It feels good for a moment, but it doesn't build anything lasting.
And deep down, we know it.

We know that no amount of "likes" or praise or feedback or admiration ever quiets the part of us that's still afraid we're not enough.

That part will never be satisfied by external approval — because it isn't asking to be validated.
It's asking to be *loved.*
By you. First.

Love doesn't need a stage.
It needs a home inside of you that says: "Even when I'm not chosen, I choose me. Even when I'm not seen, I see me. Even when I'm not praised, I'm proud of who I am."

And from that place, real love becomes possible.

Understanding Women

Symptoms of the Self-Worth Deficiency Epidemic

If low self-worth were visible, it would look like a pandemic.
Because it's everywhere — quiet, constant, and so embedded in our thinking that most women (and men) no longer see it as a problem.
They see it as personality.

But it's not personality.
It's programming.

Here's what it looks like:

- Saying sorry before you've even done anything wrong
- Feeling guilty for resting
- Talking yourself out of your own dreams
- Picking people who don't choose you
- Overgiving and resenting it
- Silencing your truth because you don't want to "cause drama"
- Needing to prove your worth through work, appearance, kindness, productivity
- Feeling anxious if someone doesn't respond immediately
- Measuring your day by how much you accomplished — not how much peace you felt

These are symptoms of an epidemic we've normalised.

We call it "being nice."
We call it "being humble."
We call it "being strong."
But underneath, it's the same story: *"I'm not enough unless..."*

Unless I'm liked.
Unless I'm chosen.
Unless I succeed.
Unless I earn it.
Unless someone tells me I'm worthy.

Understanding Women

This is not just emotional. It becomes physical.
Low self-worth manifests in exhaustion, tension, burnout, dis-ease, weight gain, disconnection.
Because your body cannot stay soft when your mind is at war with your right to exist as you are.

It becomes spiritual.
You lose faith in your intuition.
You question every decision.
You defer to others for answers you already have.

It becomes relational.
You attract mirrors of your unworthiness — people who don't see you, or people who need you to stay small.

And it becomes generational.
Because what you don't heal, you hand down.
Your children learn what worth looks like from how you treat yourself, not from what you tell them.

This is not just "a little insecurity."
It's an identity virus.

And the cost of letting it run our lives is far too high.

We don't need more women who perform perfection.
We need women who remember they are already whole — and who rise from that wholeness, not toward it.

Reclaiming Our Inner Knowing of Enoughness

You were born with it.
The knowing that you were whole.

Understanding Women

That you were worthy.
That your being — before doing, before earning, before proving — was *enough*.

Then life layered on the noise.
Expectations.
Judgments.
Systems that benefit when you doubt yourself.
Parents who passed down their unhealed beliefs.
Friends who shaped your silence.
Lovers who mirrored your wounds.

But underneath all of it, the truth never left.

You are not learning your worth.
You are remembering it.

Reclaiming your enoughness isn't about becoming someone new.
It's about returning to what has always been true about you — and deciding to live from that place.

This is an internal decision.
A quiet, radical revolution.
It begins when you stop outsourcing your value.

You stop waiting to be picked.
You stop proving your right to take up space.
You stop holding your breath for someone else's approval.

And instead, you start saying:

- *"I matter, even when I'm not producing."*
- *"I am valuable, even when I'm resting."*
- *"I am lovable, even when I'm messy."*
- *"I am enough, even when no one sees me."*

Understanding Women

Here's what that looks like in practice:

- You set boundaries that honour your body, your time, your energy.
- You say no without guilt and yes without fear.
- You stop over-explaining.
- You wear what feels like *you*, not what performs acceptability.
- You speak your truth before it becomes resentment.
- You stop shrinking when you're uncomfortable — and soften instead of harden.
- You stay rooted in your own enoughness, even when someone else's discomfort rises around it.

This is how we end the virus of low self-worth — by refusing to pass it on.
By becoming women who model what enoughness looks and feels like.
Not perfectly. Not performatively. But *genuinely*. Consistently. With grace.

Because when a woman knows she is enough, she becomes a mirror that reflects that truth back to everyone around her.

And that is the kind of healing this world is starving for.

Part Three: The Body, the Brain, and the Energy System

Chapter 7: Disconnected from Our Own Feelings

"Feeling is not weakness. It's wisdom. And the woman who knows how to stay with herself in truth will never abandon her power again."

— Heather

Why We Don't Know What We Feel Anymore

Most women are not emotionally numb by nature.
They are emotionally numb by necessity.

Because feeling — *really feeling* — in a world that rewards logic, performance, and control... is unsafe.
So we shut it down.
We suppress it, manage it, rationalise it, spiritualise it — until we no longer know what we feel at all.

We say:

- "*I'm just tired.*" When we're actually heartbroken.
- "*I'm fine.*" When we're full of rage.
- "*I don't mind.*" When we're actually deeply hurt.
- "*I'm just stressed.*" When we're not coping and haven't been for a long time.

We've been taught to *think our feelings*, not feel them.
We analyse them. We talk about them. We label them intellectually.
But the lived, felt, embodied *experience* of emotion? That's something most of us left behind years ago.

And the truth is, we had good reason.

Understanding Women

Most women didn't grow up being taught how to hold their emotions safely.
We were taught to behave, to calm down, to not make a fuss.
When we were sad, we were told to cheer up.
When we were angry, we were shamed.
When we were joyful, we were told not to get too excited.

We internalised the message: certain emotions are acceptable. The rest are dangerous.
So we adapted.
We became emotionally fluent in what made others comfortable — and emotionally mute in what made them squirm.

And now?
Now we're left with a generation of women who can't feel what they feel until it's too late.

They don't know they're angry until it explodes.
They don't know they're grieving until their body breaks down.
They don't know they're lonely until they sabotage connection.
They don't know they're overwhelmed until they're on the floor.

Not because they're broken — because they're disconnected.

Disconnected from their emotional body.
Disconnected from the intelligence of their feeling system.
Disconnected from the truth that emotion is not a weakness — it's a *compass*.

And you cannot live a full, aligned, vibrant life without access to that compass.

This chapter is not here to teach you how to control your emotions.
It's here to help you reclaim them.
To bring you back into contact with what you actually feel — not what you think you *should* feel.

Because your emotional truth is not dangerous.
It is the doorway home.

Understanding Women

The Freeze Between Body and Mind

There is a space between your thoughts and your body — a gap most women live inside without even knowing it.

It's a freeze state.
Not quite shut down, not quite awake.
It's the place where you know something is off, but you can't put your finger on it.
Where you're functioning on the outside, but frozen on the inside.

You laugh when you're supposed to.
You smile for photos.
You say all the right things.
But deep down, you're not there.
Not *fully*. Not *in your body*. Not *alive*.

This is not laziness. This is not failure.
This is what happens when the body and the mind stop trusting each other.

When you live in survival mode long enough, your body learns not to send you emotional signals anymore — because you don't respond to them, or you punish them, or you override them with logic. So the feelings get buried. The body stops talking. Or worse — it starts screaming in other ways:

- Anxiety
- Tight chest
- Digestive issues
- Weight fluctuations
- Fatigue
- Restlessness
- Shallow breath
- Illness and dis-ease
- A constant hum of "*something's not right*" without a clear cause

These are not random. These are *frozen emotions* trying to surface.

Women in freeze states often appear high-functioning, even successful.
They can run companies, manage households, hold it all together.

But they are *dissociated*.
From their joy.
From their grief.
From their needs.
From their bodies.
From the very centre of who they are.

This isn't just emotional disconnection — it's an energetic one.
Because when we disconnect from our emotional body, we also disconnect from our *energy system*.
And when the energy system is numb, intuition dims. Creativity shuts down. Sensuality flattens. Life becomes something to manage, not something to *feel*.

The freeze state is not the enemy — it's a survival mechanism.
But survival is not your destiny.

You are here to *thrive*.
To feel fully.
To *live in your body*, not just drag it behind you.

And to do that, we have to start rebuilding the bridge between the head and the heart.
Between the thoughts and the sensations.
Between the woman who's performing — and the woman who's actually present.

Learning to Name, Feel, and Stay With Emotion

Healing begins with language.
Not fancy language. Not spiritual language.
Just *truthful* language.

Because if you can't name what you feel, you can't hold it.
And if you can't hold it, you'll try to escape it, suppress it, project it, or perform over it.

Naming is the first thread of reconnection.
But it must be simple.

Not: "*I feel energetically imbalanced due to relational turbulence.*"
But:

- "*I feel sad.*"
- "*I feel scared.*"
- "*I feel angry.*"
- "*I feel lonely.*"
- "*I feel rejected.*"

Name it. Without judging it. Without fixing it. Without making it wrong.
That alone is a radical act.

Once you've named it, the next step is to *feel it*.
Not in your head. In your body.

Where does it live?
What does it feel like — tightness, heat, hollowness, pressure, cold?
Can you breathe into it without pushing it away?

Most of us were never taught how to do this.
We were taught to rush to solutions.
To make it better.
To reframe it, rationalise it, distract from it, spiritualise it.

But real feeling is not dramatic. It's *honest*.
It's letting the sensation pass through you instead of resisting or reacting to it.

You don't need to *understand* your feelings right away.
You need to *allow* them.

And finally: *stay with it.*

This is where the nervous system begins to rewire.
When you prove to yourself that you don't have to run.

You don't need to run from sadness.
You don't need to run from fear.
You don't need to run from grief, loneliness, shame, disappointment, confusion.

You can stay. You can hold. You can breathe.
You can feel the waves and let them move through without drowning in them.

This is emotional maturity.
This is the feminine nervous system coming back online.

You don't need to be a master of emotion.
You just need to stop abandoning yourself in moments when you most need to be held.

And the woman who can stay with herself — without judgment, without collapse — is a woman who has returned to her *true* power.

From Suppression to Soulful Sensation

Emotions aren't meant to be stored.
They're meant to be *felt*.
They are energy in motion — designed to move through the body like weather across a sky.
But when we suppress them, that energy gets trapped. And trapped energy becomes pain.

Emotional pain.
Physical pain.
Energetic stagnation.
Mental confusion.
Spiritual disconnection.

Understanding Women

Suppression always has a cost.

The woman who suppresses her feelings becomes a stranger to herself.
She looks whole on the outside.
But inside, there's a backlog of unshed tears, unfelt rage, unheard grief.
She starts to live in patterns, not presence.
She reacts instead of responds.
She disconnects from intimacy, from pleasure, from life.
And often, she doesn't even realise it.

Because suppression becomes normal.
Expected. Praised.
She's strong.
She's easy.
She doesn't cause trouble.
She doesn't need much.
But she's *gone*. She's *hollowed out* by the very feelings she's been taught to silence.

So what does it look like to live in soulful sensation instead?

It looks like a woman who is *in her body*.
Not because she's mastered some mystical technique — but because she's present.

- She notices what she feels as it arises.
- She breathes instead of flinching.
- She doesn't pretend to be fine when she's not.
- She expresses what's true, not what's polite.
- She's not ruled by emotion — but she's not ruled by resistance either.
- She's fluid. Alive. Honest.

And deeply *safe to herself.*

Soulful sensation isn't about feeling everything all the time.
It's about being in relationship with what's real.

Understanding Women

It's about *listening* instead of silencing.
Trusting instead of controlling.
Flowing instead of freezing.

This isn't weakness. It's feminine intelligence in motion.

You don't have to live in suppression anymore.
You don't have to manage your emotions like a crisis.
You don't have to keep stuffing down what your soul is begging you to feel.

You are safe to feel.
You are safe to express.
You are safe to be *with yourself* in the truth of the moment.

And when you return to that truth, your energy unfreezes.
Your body breathes.
Your clarity sharpens.
Your life begins to move again — from survival to sensation, from performance to presence.

You were never meant to be numb.
You were meant to feel.
And feeling — fully, soulfully — is not your weakness.
It's your way home.

Understanding Women

Chapter 8: The Parasympathetic Path to Peace

"Peace is not a place you reach. It's a rhythm your body remembers, when you stop asking it to prove anything."

— **Heather**

Understanding the Brain's Relationship to Safety

Your nervous system is not just a background function.
It is the *landscape of your entire inner world*.
And at the core of it lies one quiet, powerful question that runs through your brain all day, every day:

"Am I safe?"

This question governs everything — how you think, how you react, how you speak, how you rest, how you relate to others, and most of all, how deeply you can *feel*. Because if the brain doesn't register safety, your body will not relax. And if your body cannot relax, your soul cannot land.

Most women don't feel safe — not truly.
They feel alert. Productive. Busy. Accommodating.
But they don't feel safe to slow down.
Safe to speak honestly.
Safe to feel their feelings.
Safe to soften into the moment without scanning it for danger, judgment, or obligation.

That's because most women are living from their sympathetic nervous system — the part of the body designed for protection, not peace.

Understanding Women

Fight. Flight. Freeze. Fawn.
Always on. Always planning. Always managing.
Even in stillness, the inner world is tight, braced, alert.

And it's exhausting.

The parasympathetic nervous system is your pathway home.
This is the part of the body that governs *rest, repair, digest, feel, connect, trust.*
It is the feminine nervous system in motion.
Soft. Receptive. Still. Clear. Present.
It is where true emotion gets integrated, not just felt.
Where clarity returns. Where healing can begin.

But here's the hard truth:
You can't access it through force.
You can't *think* your way into calm.
You *feel* your way there.

You don't drop into the parasympathetic through effort.
You drop in through trust.

So when we talk about emotional safety, nervous system healing, or coming back into alignment, what we're really saying is:

"I am ready to stop bracing for impact — and start building a relationship with the part of me that knows how to receive life in peace."

This isn't a luxury. It's *essential*.

Because until your brain believes you are safe, it will keep choosing survival — even when the danger is long gone.

Understanding Women

Rewiring Through Self-Worth Affirmations and Soothing Practices

The nervous system doesn't speak words.
It speaks sensation.
It speaks repetition.
It speaks in felt experiences of safety or danger.

Which means you can't just tell your system you're safe — you have to *show* it.

This is where self-worth affirmations and soothing practices become more than nice ideas.
They become rewiring tools.
Not because they instantly fix anything, but because they begin to shift your *baseline experience* of being in your body.

Affirmations are not just positive thinking.
When done right, they are slow, deliberate *re-education* for the subconscious mind.
They are a way of introducing new truths — truths your body may not yet believe, but is willing to begin learning.

When paired with the right tone, breath, and repetition, affirmations help teach the brain:

- *"I am safe now."*
- *"I don't have to perform to belong."*
- *"I am worthy of love, even when I'm still learning."*
- *"It's okay to rest. Nothing is collapsing."*
- *"I trust myself to feel this."*

These are not fluffy words.
These are neural instructions.

And with time, the brain starts to believe what the heart has known all along: *"You are enough, even here. Even now."*

But affirmations alone aren't enough. They need to be paired with soothing practices that ground the nervous system in real-time experience.

Simple practices, repeated consistently, are the most powerful:

- Deep, slow breathing into your belly
- Placing a hand on your heart or lower belly and saying, "I've got you"
- Gentle movement that feels nourishing, not punishing
- Sitting with yourself without a task — just to be
- Touching your skin with care, as a reminder that your body is safe
- Speaking aloud a loving truth when the inner critic rises

These are rituals of *re-safetying*.
Not just tools to manage anxiety — but invitations back into the parasympathetic state where your system says, "*I can soften. I don't have to be on alert anymore.*"

You are not broken for feeling frazzled.
You are not weak for needing comfort.
You are not failing if it takes time to unwind.

Your nervous system is listening.
And every time you choose softness over self-judgment, presence over pressure, compassion over criticism — you are teaching your entire being that peace *is possible.*

The Role of the Gut, Heart, and Enteric Intelligence

Most people think their thinking happens only in the brain.
But that's not where your deepest wisdom lives.
It lives in the *network* of your body.

Your nervous system is intelligent.
But it's not just *one* system — it's a *conversation* happening across three main centres:
The gut, the heart, and the brain.

And for most people, that conversation has been disrupted.
Because we were taught to trust our thoughts, but not our feelings.
To obey logic, but ignore instinct.
To perform for approval, but never pause to check in with our own truth.

Let's begin with the gut.
This is where the enteric nervous system lives — often called "the second brain."
It holds over 500 million neurons, and it speaks in sensation, not sentence.

That "gut feeling" you get?
It's not emotional fluff.
It's real, physiological guidance.
And when you're dysregulated, disconnected, or living in stress for too long, that connection becomes foggy or completely numb.

When the gut is ignored, our boundaries collapse.
We override what we know.
We say yes when everything in us says no.
We stay when we know we should go.
We tolerate things that make us sick.

But when we start to *listen*, the gut recalibrates.
And we begin to trust again — not from fear, but from *truth*.

Then, there's the heart.
Not just the seat of emotion, but a powerhouse of energy and coherence.

The heart sends more signals to the brain than the brain sends to the heart.
And when your heart is in harmony — when it feels safe, open, and steady — it actually changes the way your brain processes stress, fear, and connection.

Your heart can lead.
But only when it's allowed to *feel*.
To grieve. To soften. To beat in time with your emotional truth, not your performance.

This is why so many women feel disconnected in relationships — they're leading from logic, but their heart has shut down.

And finally, the brain.
Brilliant. Fast. Capable.
But without input from the gut and the heart, it's a master without counsel.

This is what creates imbalance:

- A woman living only in her head.
- Disconnected from her inner compass.
- Running her life on strategy instead of sensitivity.
- Making choices based on fear, pattern, or productivity — because her deeper systems have gone offline.

Reconnecting with your enteric intelligence doesn't require you to study.
It requires you to *feel*.
To soften.
To breathe.
To pause long enough to notice: "*What is my gut saying? What is my heart needing? What is my body trying to tell me?*"

You were never meant to live only from your mind.
You are a system of wisdom.
And when these centres begin to speak to one another again — gut, heart, brain — you stop reacting, and you start *responding* from your whole self.

Daily Rituals That Reconnect You to Your Calm

Peace isn't something you wait for.
It's something you *practice*.

And for the feminine nervous system to thrive, it must be invited — daily — into states of calm, trust, and soft awareness.

These rituals aren't about perfection.
They're about presence.
Each one is a doorway. A signal to your body: "*You are safe now. You can rest. You can return.*"

Here are six powerful, simple daily rituals to reconnect you to your calm:

1. Start with Silence

Before the world reaches for you, sit with yourself.
Even just for three minutes.
No phone. No plans. No pressure.

Close your eyes.
Place your hands on your body — your belly, your chest, your thighs.
Breathe. Let silence hold you.

This tells your system: "*We don't start the day in urgency. We begin in presence.*"

2. Anchor with Breath Throughout the Day

Any time you feel tension rising — pause.
Breathe in through your nose.
Exhale slowly and audibly through your mouth.
Three times. No rush.

Your breath is your bridge back to now.
It grounds you. It tells your body, "*We're safe.*"

3. Ground Through Touch

The body softens with touch — especially your own.

- Stroke your arms gently.
- Place a hand over your heart or womb.
- Massage your scalp slowly.

- Lay your palms on your thighs and feel your presence.

Touch says: "*You're here. You matter. I see you.*"

4. End the Day with a Self-Worth Statement

As you lie down, speak something true and kind to yourself.
Let it be simple, embodied, and real:

- *"I did enough today."*
- *"I'm allowed to rest now."*
- *"I am proud of how I showed up."*

Let it be the last voice your nervous system hears.

5. Ritualise One Act of Receiving Daily

Choose one thing, every day, that is just for you.
Not to achieve. Not to impress. Not to perform. Just to *receive*.

- A slow walk in nature
- A hot bath with music
- A quiet tea with no tasks
- A moment of stillness with your hand over your heart

Receiving tells your system: "*Life can feel good.*"

6. Five Minutes of Self-Worth Talk (Rewiring Through Repetition)

Set a timer. Five minutes.
Stand, sit, or lie down — however your body feels safe.
Breathe gently and begin to speak your truth out loud:

- *"I am enough."*
- *"I am safe to be seen."*
- *"I am clever, kind, radiant, and real."*

- *"I am worthy of love just as I am."*
- *"I do not need to perform to belong."*
- *"I have the right to feel joy and live in truth."*
- *"I am not too much. I am finally just enough."*

Speak slowly. Let your words land.
This isn't performance. This is programming — rewriting your inner code, breath by breath.

Say it until your body listens. Until your brain softens. Until your soul believes you again.

These rituals are not about checking boxes.
They're about *changing your relationship with yourself.*
They're about teaching your system, again and again, *"I will not abandon you. I am here. And we are safe now."*

This is the parasympathetic path to peace.
And it begins, always, with you.

Understanding Women

Chapter 9: Subtle Energy, Environmental Influence, and the Mirror Effect

"Your presence is not passive. It's a frequency. Every room you enter, you're either leaking, leading, or lifting. Choose with care."

— **Heather**

How Energy Moves Through and Around You

You don't just live in the world.
You live in a *field*.
A field of energy that you carry, emit, absorb, and respond to — constantly.

And every part of you is involved.
Your thoughts carry energy.
Your emotions carry energy.
Your words, your breath, your posture, your intentions — all of it is *energetically active.*

Energy is not abstract. It is practical, measurable, and *personal.*
It is the atmosphere of your life.

Most women were never taught to notice this.
They're taught to focus on what's visible — behaviour, achievement, appearance.
But what actually shapes your day, your interactions, and your self-concept is what's happening in the invisible — the *feeling* beneath the words, the *vibration* behind the presence, the *intention* inside the exchange.

You've felt this.

Understanding Women

- The way someone's energy walks into a room before their body does.
- The heaviness that lingers after an argument — even in silence.
- The tingling you feel when someone is thinking of you.
- The exhaustion after being around someone who constantly complains.
- The subtle peace of being near someone whose energy is calm and steady.

You are not imagining these things.
You are *reading* energy.
Because energy moves *through* you as much as it moves *around* you.

And here's the part we're rarely taught:
You don't just absorb energy. You also *emit* it.

Your energy field is not passive — it's *participatory*.
You're not just influenced by your environment. You are actively shaping it with your presence.

Every thought you feed becomes frequency.
Every belief you carry lives in your body and radiates outward.
Every emotion you feel but do not process gets stored in your field like static.

And when your field is congested, unprocessed, or scattered — your clarity dims.
You attract more of what reflects your confusion.
You feel other people's emotions as your own.
You lose sight of your own centre because your system is overwhelmed by input.

But when your energy is clear — when you are present, grounded, honest, and aligned — everything changes.

You no longer chase.
You no longer leak.
You no longer lose yourself in other people's moods or needs.

Instead, you become magnetic.
Steady.

Understanding Women

You hold your own frequency like a lighthouse — and the right people, opportunities, and insights start arriving without you needing to grasp for them.

Because energy speaks before action ever does.

Learning how energy moves isn't about becoming mystical.
It's about becoming *sovereign* in your space.
It's about finally realising: *you are not just a body walking through the world — you are an energy field shaping it.*

And when you learn how to tend that field, you stop being at the mercy of your environment, and start becoming the author of your experience.

The Influence of Relationships, Spaces, and Beliefs

You don't just absorb energy from the air.
You absorb it from the people around you.
And not just from what they say — but from *how* they show up in your field.

Some relationships feel like nourishment.
Some feel like static.
Some feel like storms.

This isn't always about who they are — it's about how *you* and *they* interact energetically.
Because we're not just exchanging words. We're exchanging frequency.

When someone shares with presence, awareness, and openness, it creates energetic harmony.
But when someone demands attention, over-identifies with their suffering, or assumes the centre of the room — it becomes *energetically invasive.*

And this is where we need to speak plainly about something that's rarely named:
The ego doesn't just want to be important. It wants to be the best.
And when it can't be the best at something noble, it often settles for being the best at something destructive.

Understanding Women

- The best at being the most sensitive.
- The most spiritual.
- The most traumatised.
- The most misunderstood.
- The most giving, selfless, exhausted.
- The most abandoned.
- The most psychic.
- The most generous with nothing left in the tank.
- The most "*real.*"

And that might sound harmless, but energetically — it's *chaotic.*
Because those ego patterns leak energy into every space they enter.

Here's what it looks like in real life:

Someone loudly declares, "*I'm an empath,*" on a group call — oblivious to the sensitivity of everyone else in the room.
Someone dumps their life story on you without once checking whether you have the capacity to receive it.
Someone lashes out because you didn't show up the way they expected you to — how dare you not perform for them?
Someone announces "*I'm just like you*" when they barely know you, but they have compared themselves and want to "rank" their capability alongside or above yours.
Someone claims they are a "healer" but they have so many unhealed wounds that their audience becomes a conduit for pain sharing.
Someone spiritualises their need for control and calls it "guidance."

This behaviour is not only draining — it's energetically aggressive.

Because it's not true connection.
It's a *one-way projection.*
And projections, when unowned, become invasions.

Understanding Women

Women must begin to take responsibility for the way they show up energetically in community, in friendship, in spiritual circles, and in mentorship.

Sensitivity without self-awareness is not a gift — it's a storm.
And entitlement wrapped in emotional language is still control.

It doesn't make you powerful to be the one who feels the most.
It makes you powerful to be the one who can hold what she feels, *without throwing it at other people*.

This is why energetic hygiene matters.
Because your presence has impact.
And if you don't know how to self-regulate, self-contain, and self-soothe — you will unconsciously make other people responsible for your experience.

And that is not love. That is not connection. That is not sovereignty.
That is ego in disguise.

What We Attract, What We Project, and What We Absorb

We are magnetic. Not metaphorically — energetically.
We draw in what matches our frequency, we repel what doesn't, and we absorb more than we realise.

And if we're not conscious of this, we start mistaking our *energy field* for our *personality*.

But here's the truth:

- You attract what reflects what you believe you deserve.
- You project what you haven't yet accepted in yourself.
- You absorb what you don't yet know how to say no to.

What You Attract

You don't attract what you want — you attract what you *believe you are available for*.

Understanding Women

If you believe love requires self-abandonment, you'll attract partners who demand that of you.
If you believe success means burnout, you'll attract opportunities that exhaust you.
If you believe women are untrustworthy, you'll attract female friendships that confirm the story.

Energy doesn't follow desire. It follows *belief.*

What You Project

Whatever you haven't healed or integrated in yourself, you'll end up projecting onto others.

You'll call someone arrogant when what you're really seeing is confidence you haven't yet allowed yourself to claim.
You'll judge someone for being emotional when what you're really reacting to is your own shutdown.
You'll accuse someone of abandoning you when what you're really facing is your own self-abandonment.

Projection is not the enemy.
It's the invitation.

It says: "*This is yours to look at.*"

What You Absorb

If you don't have energetic boundaries, you'll start picking up other people's emotions, beliefs, expectations, and moods — and thinking they're your own.

You'll feel anxious and not know why.
You'll feel depleted around someone and think *you're* the problem.
You'll take on guilt that was never yours.
You'll contort yourself to avoid someone else's disapproval.
And you'll call that connection — but it's not. It's *entanglement.*

Understanding Women

Women who absorb too much are often praised for being kind, empathetic, or "easygoing."
But often, what they really are... is porous.
And being porous doesn't make you loving.
It makes you leaky.

If you want to change your experience of life, you must stop blaming your environment and start understanding how you interact with it:

- *"What am I believing that's creating this pattern?"*
- *"What am I projecting that I need to own?"*
- *"What am I absorbing that I never agreed to carry?"*

You don't need to be perfect to clean up your energy.
You just need to be *honest*.

And from that honesty, you can start to tend the field that you live in — not with fear or control, but with care.

Tending the Garden of Your Inner and Outer Environment

Your energy field is like a garden.
Whatever you feed, grows.
Whatever you neglect, withers.
And whatever you allow in — whether consciously or unconsciously — takes root.

Most women tend to everyone else's garden but forget to care for their own.
They pull weeds from other people's lives.
They plant seeds in relationships that don't water them back.
They stand in overgrown spaces filled with judgment, chaos, and noise — and wonder why they feel depleted.

But here's the truth:
You are allowed to cultivate your own field.

Understanding Women

You are allowed to choose what grows around you and within you.
You are allowed to make your environment sacred — not because it's perfect, but because *you are finally paying attention.*

This begins inside.

Tending your inner environment means noticing the energy you carry throughout the day:

- Are your thoughts kind or critical?
- Are your emotions allowed to move or are they stuffed down?
- Is your inner dialogue one of pressure, or one of presence?
- Do you speak to yourself like someone you love, or someone you tolerate?

Your inner world becomes your outer experience.
Every belief, every emotion, every unspoken truth has a frequency.
And that frequency colours every conversation, decision, and connection.

If your inner garden is full of weeds, self-doubt, and resentment — of course you're exhausted.
You're growing depletion.
But if you begin to plant peace, worthiness, clarity, and compassion — *you will feel that shift.*
And so will everyone around you.

Then there's your outer environment.

The people. The spaces. The online worlds. The energetic contracts you keep out of guilt or habit.

Ask yourself:

- *"Does this space support my truth, or silence it?"*
- *"Does this relationship respect my energy, or rely on me abandoning myself?"*
- *"Does this input lift me, or leave me more confused?"*
- *"Am I walking into rooms that require me to shrink — or to shine?"*

Understanding Women

Tending your outer world doesn't mean isolating yourself or cutting everyone off.
It means choosing environments that match your healing — not your fear.

And finally, this:
The more carefully you tend to your energy, the more obvious it becomes *what doesn't belong there.*
This is not arrogance. This is discernment.

You are not here to be everything for everyone.
You are here to be *aligned.*
And alignment only grows in a field that is nurtured, not neglected.

Tend to your garden with presence, with honesty, and with care.
Not because the world will change around you — but because *you will.*

And when you do, the world cannot help but meet you in your new frequency.

Part Four: The Five Ego Fears and the Feminine Soul

Understanding Women

Chapter 10: The Masculine Energy Fear Matrix

The ego doesn't fear what's happening. It fears what might. Until you bring yourself into the present, fear will keep dragging you out of the life that's actually here."

— ***Heather***

Death, Illness, Shame, Rejection, Loss of Freedom

There are five core fears that govern almost every unconscious reaction in the human experience:

Death. Illness. Shame. Rejection. Loss of Freedom.

They don't always show up in obvious ways.
They disguise themselves in the cracks of our lives — through control, avoidance, overthinking, perfectionism, performance, people-pleasing, silence, rage, collapse.

And they all belong to the ego.

Because the ego is the part of us designed for survival.
Its job is not to evolve you. Its job is to protect you.
And it does that by projecting fear into the future and rehearsing pain that hasn't happened yet.

These fears are not *felt* in the present moment.
They are *imagined*.
They are perceived threats — visions of what might happen, not truths of what *is*.

- You're not dying — you're afraid of the loss of control.

Understanding Women

- You're not being rejected — you're afraid that if someone doesn't approve of you, you don't exist.
- You're not ashamed — you're afraid that if someone sees the real you, they'll leave.
- You're not afraid of being sick — you're afraid of what illness represents: weakness, collapse, death, being forgotten.
- You're not trapped — you're afraid of responsibility, failure, exposure, or emotional stillness.

The ego doesn't deal in facts. It deals in protection.
And it will use fear — every *time* — to keep you from expanding.

1. Fear of Death

This is the root fear.
Not just of physical death, but ego death.
The fear of ending. Of change. Of being erased. Of the unknown.

It shows up in how we resist growth, transformation, silence, surrender.
It's what keeps us chasing safety instead of making peace.

2. Fear of Illness

This is the fear of fragility.
The fear of breaking down. Of being dependent. Of being seen as weak.
It can lead to obsession with control, health perfectionism, denial, or a total disconnect from the body.

The body becomes the battlefield — not a home.

3. Fear of Shame

One of the most painful.
The fear of being seen and judged.
Of being humiliated. Of not being enough.

It keeps women hiding.
Over-performing.
Trying to pre-empt being "too much" or "not enough" by shape-shifting constantly.

Shame says: "*If they see who I really am, I will be cast out.*"
So the mask stays on.

4. Fear of Rejection

This fear controls so many decisions.
We say yes when we mean no.
We overgive. We silence our truth. We dim our light.
Because the ego says: "*If you don't belong, you won't survive.*"

It makes connection feel conditional.
It makes authenticity feel dangerous.

5. Fear of Loss of Freedom

This is the fear of being trapped.
In relationships. In jobs. In family. In choices.
Often, it's rooted in early trauma where freedom was taken away or where love came with control.

It can make commitment feel like confinement.
It can make intimacy feel like suffocation.
It's not freedom we fear losing — it's *sovereignty*.

These fears are not truth.
They are projections.
Echoes of past pain. Forecasts of imagined danger.
They are ego-based attempts to stay safe — by never stepping into the unknown.

But here's the paradox:
The more we live in fear, the less safe we actually feel.

And the less safe we feel, the more the ego takes control.
It's a loop.

The only way out is *presence*.

Because fear doesn't live in the now.
It only lives in memory and projection.
And when you bring yourself *into your body, into this moment*, fear has nowhere to land.

How These Fears Live in the Nervous System

Fear isn't just a mental concept.
It's a physiological imprint.
It lives in your nervous system — deeply, memorised, and often unconscious.

You don't have to *think* a fearful thought to *feel* fear.
The body remembers before the brain does.

That's why sometimes you feel anxious for "no reason."
Or you freeze in situations that seem safe.
Or you find yourself reactive, shut down, or overfunctioning before you've even had time to think.

This is not failure. This is patterning.
Your nervous system has been taught, over time, what feels safe — and what doesn't.
And most of those teachings were not conscious.
They were inherited, modelled, and imprinted.

Let's break it down simply:

- When your body experiences fear, it shifts into survival mode.
- Your sympathetic nervous system activates: fight, flight, freeze, or fawn.
- Blood flow leaves your digestive system and moves to your limbs.
- Your breath shortens. Your heart rate quickens. Your vision narrows.

- Your ability to think clearly disappears — because survival doesn't require reflection. It requires reaction.

This is exactly how fear bypasses logic.
It doesn't wait for your thoughts. It *takes over your system.*
And once it does, your reactions are no longer aligned with who you truly are.
They are controlled by who you had to be, to stay safe.

Each of the five masculine energy-based fears has its own energetic signature in the body:

- Fear of death → Panic, overwhelm, chronic hyper-vigilance
- Fear of illness → Health anxiety, obsessive body scanning, hyper-control over food or rest
- Fear of shame → Contracted chest, shallow breath, hypersensitivity to judgment
- Fear of rejection → People-pleasing, overexplaining, inability to say no
- Fear of loss of freedom → Restlessness, emotional avoidance, inability to commit

These responses may have once protected you.
But if they are still running your system now, they are likely keeping you small.

Fear isn't bad.
It's *honest.*
It tells us what the body still believes is dangerous.

But when those beliefs are outdated, inherited, or based on trauma — we end up living a life shaped by old wounds, not current reality.

This is why healing the internal feminine energy balance requires us to not just understand fear — but to *work with it* inside the body.

Because until the nervous system feels safe, the soul cannot fully land.

Understanding Women

Using Masculine Energy to Recognise and Contain Fear

Feminine energy is fluid, emotional, intuitive, and deeply connected to the present moment.
But when fear enters the system, the feminine often gets swept up, overwhelmed, scattered — or completely shut down.

This is where we need to bring in masculine energy.
Not dominance. Not force.
But the *healthy*, grounded, steady container that allows fear to be seen, named, and held — without letting it run the show.

Masculine energy, when healed, doesn't suppress fear.
It recognises it.
It says, "*I see you. I've got you. We are safe.*"
It doesn't need to fix. It just *holds* — firm, unshaken, clear.

This is a massive key in learning to regulate your nervous system:
You don't need to stop being afraid.
You need to *meet fear with structure*.

Fear is messy. Masculine energy offers direction.
Fear spirals. Masculine energy grounds.
Fear floods. Masculine energy becomes the levee.
Not to block the emotion, but to keep it *contained enough* that the feminine can still feel, and the system can stay *present*.

So what does this actually look like?

It looks like:

- Naming the fear out loud: "*I feel scared of being judged right now.*"
- Setting a clear intention: "*I am not abandoning myself in this moment.*"

- Placing a hand on your belly and slowing the breath: "*I am here. This feeling is safe to move.*"
- Keeping the body still while the emotion rises — offering it *structure* rather than chaos.
- Saying to yourself: "*This fear is old. I choose to be here now.*"

This is masculine energy in practice:
Present, clean, clear, loving.

When the feminine meets fear alone, she either collapses or goes into emotional survival. When the feminine meets fear *held* by the masculine — internally or externally — she can stay soft and awake without abandoning herself.

You can give that to yourself.
You don't need someone else to hold it for you.

The feminine in you deserves to be protected by the masculine in you. And until that partnership exists internally, your system will keep looking for safety outside itself — where it can never be guaranteed.

This is the gift of balanced inner energy:
Masculine energy offers the perimeter.
Feminine energy rests in the centre.
And in that relationship, *fear no longer has to lead.*

Freeing the Body from Generational Fear Programming

The fears you carry didn't start with you.

They were passed down — coded into your body, your behaviour, your nervous system — like invisible blueprints.
You inherited them not just through stories and language, but through energy, through tone, through silence, through what wasn't said, but deeply felt.

Understanding Women

Fear has a lineage.

- The fear of being too much.
- The fear of not being chosen.
- The fear of being left behind.
- The fear of being punished for being visible.
- The fear of softness, of stillness, of wanting more.

These are ancestral echoes.
They live in the body like muscle memory.

This is why healing isn't just mindset work.
It's body work.
It's energy work.
It's the quiet, consistent process of teaching your nervous system that you are no longer in the conditions that created the fear.

You are not your mother's fear.
You are not your grandmother's suppression.
You are not your family's pattern of silence, shame, collapse, or survival.

You carry it — but you do not have to continue it.

Freeing the body from generational fear means becoming conscious of what you're holding that was never yours to begin with.

Ask yourself:

- *"Where did I learn that I can't be safe and soft at the same time?"*
- *"Who told me I had to choose between love and freedom?"*
- *"What fear do I carry that actually belongs to another generation?"*
- *"What reaction in my body isn't about now — but about then?"*

And then, bring it into presence. Into compassion. Into *choice*.

Understanding Women

Your body has an incredible capacity to let go of fear when it feels safe, seen, and re-supported.
This is where the masculine energy returns — not as domination, but as containment.
The energy that says: "*This ends with me.*"

When you start living from now, not from *then*, everything shifts.

Your decisions become clearer.
Your relationships become cleaner.
Your breath returns.
Your soul softens.

You cannot fully embody your feminine self while living in a fear-conditioned body.
And you don't have to keep fear as your compass.
It was never meant to be the driver.
It was only meant to be a signal.

Now that you see it — you can choose differently.
And that choice *is freedom*.

Understanding Women

Chapter 11: The Feminine Soul's One Deep Longing

"Your soul is not starving because you're broken. It's starving because you keep feeding the world before you feed yourself."

— **Heather**

The Fear of Not Being Ourselves

There is one fear that lives deeper than all the rest.
It doesn't shout like shame.
It doesn't panic like rejection.
It doesn't freeze like loss or death.

It aches.
Quietly. Constantly.
A low hum beneath the surface of every compromise, every mask, every time we twist ourselves just slightly out of shape.

It's the fear of this:
"If I am truly myself, I won't be loved."

This is the fear that keeps women disconnected from their own souls.
Because the soul doesn't perform.
The soul doesn't posture.
The soul doesn't prove.
The soul simply *is*.

And if you've been taught that "being" is not enough — only effort, achievement, pleasing, perfection, or usefulness — then you've learned to *hide* the very essence of who you are in order to be accepted.

That's not survival.
That's starvation.

We all want to be loved for who we really are.
But here's the part we must be brave enough to hear:

You cannot be loved for who you are while you're still hiding her.
You cannot wait for someone else to give you permission.
You cannot outsource the job of accepting yourself.
You cannot keep saying, "*I want to be loved for who I am,*" while continuing to be who you're not just to earn that love.

That's not intimacy. That's negotiation.
And the soul doesn't deal in bargains.
It deals in truth.

So the deepest longing of the feminine soul is not just to be loved.
It's to be *loved while being fully herself.*
Messy. Unfiltered. Unapologetic. Expressed. Whole. Honest. Tender. Fierce. Free.

But here's the truth most people never realise:

You must go first.

You must be the one to say:

- "*I accept myself.*"
- "*I choose myself.*"
- "*I love myself not because someone else told me I was worthy — but because I know who I am.*"

If you don't go first, no one else can meet you there.
Because the way you love yourself sets the standard for every relationship in your life.

Understanding Women

This chapter is not about waiting for someone to see you.
It's about you seeing *you*.

Because when a woman returns to the truth of who she is — beneath the masks, the fear, the pressure to be palatable — *she becomes magnetic.*
She becomes *free.*
She becomes *whole.*

And love, from others, becomes a reflection of what already lives within her — not a lifeline to prove she deserves to exist.

Why the Soul Needs Permission to Lead

Your soul has always been trying to lead.
It's not new. It's not distant. It's not silent.

It speaks through longing.
It speaks through discomfort.
It speaks through the ache you feel when you're living a life that looks fine on the outside but feels empty on the inside.

But here's the thing — the soul cannot override your free will.
It cannot force its way in.
It needs your *invitation.*

And most women have never given it.

Why?

Because the soul doesn't speak the language of performance.
It doesn't care how you look.
It doesn't care what they think.
It doesn't care how much you earn, how many followers you have, or how "productive" your day was.

Understanding Women

The soul leads with feeling.
The soul leads with truth.
The soul leads with presence, not pressure.
With alignment, not obligation.

And that kind of leadership requires trust.
It requires a woman to *stop outsourcing her value* and begin listening inward, deeply, daily.

But most women are waiting.
Waiting to feel ready.
Waiting for the right sign.
Waiting for someone else to go first.
Waiting for a guarantee that if they follow the soul, nothing will be lost.

But the soul doesn't promise safety.
It promises *truth*.
It promises *liberation*.
It promises that if you follow it — you'll finally feel *alive*.

But only if you let it lead.

So ask yourself:

- *"Where am I still leading from fear instead of truth?"*
- *"Where am I asking for guidance, but resisting what I already know?"*
- *"Where am I still demanding proof, instead of giving myself permission?"*

The soul doesn't need to be chased.
It just needs to be *trusted*.
It needs space.
It needs silence.
It needs your yes.

Because until you say, "*You can lead now*," it will keep whispering into the background noise of your life — and you will keep mistaking your longing for confusion.

The soul doesn't need your perfection.
It needs your *participation*.

Give it that, and you'll find that everything you were chasing begins to turn around and walk toward you.

Recognising the Feeling of Soul Starvation

Soul starvation is quiet.
It doesn't announce itself with sirens.
It creeps in through the gaps between what you *do* and who you really *are*.

You don't always notice it right away.
You're too busy keeping everything together.
Smiling. Serving. Achieving. Showing up.
You're ticking every box except the one that says "*true self.*"

And then it hits — subtly at first:

- That moment of hollowness in a room full of people.
- The sense that something's missing, even though your life is "fine."
- The exhaustion that no amount of sleep seems to fix.
- The loop of "Why does this still not feel like enough?"

This is not depression.
This is not failure.
This is your soul trying to get your attention.

A soul-starved woman often looks like she's doing well.
Because she's trying to fill the void with everything except what actually nourishes her.

Understanding Women

She over-gives.
She over-performs.
She becomes "low maintenance" to the world and high-pressure to herself.
She silences her longings and calls it humility.
She keeps people close by hiding the parts of her that would truly connect them.

But underneath the surface — she's shrinking.
She's aching.
She's starving.

Here's how you know the soul is being starved:

- You lose interest in what once lit you up.
- You start resenting people who seem more free than you.
- You judge others' expression because it mirrors your own suppression.
- You feel disconnected from your own body, your own desire, your own essence.
- You crave something but can't name it — because it's not a thing. It's you.

It's not the job. It's not the partner. It's not the schedule.
It's the fact that your soul hasn't been fed in weeks, months, maybe years.

And now she's whispering: "*Remember me. I'm still here.*"

Soul starvation doesn't require a breakdown to be addressed.
It just needs one honest moment:
A breath. A pause. A return.

To stop and say:
"*What is mine to carry? And what is mine to create?*"
"*What part of me have I locked away, waiting for someone else to open the door?*"

Here's the truth: No one is coming to feed the parts of you you've abandoned.
That is your work. That is your gift.
And when you begin feeding your soul again, everything begins to bloom from the inside out.

Understanding Women

Feeding the Soul Through Creativity, Rest, and Connection

The soul doesn't need performance.
It needs permission.
It needs presence.
And it needs nourishment — not through pressure or doing more, but through *returning* to what is already true.

You don't feed the soul by ticking another box.
You feed the soul by letting yourself be *human*.
Creative. Rested. Connected. Unarmoured. Awake.

Feed Your Soul Through Creativity

Your soul is not fed by logic. It is fed by *expression* — especially unproductive, unscheduled, unjudged expression.

Write, paint, dance, sing, build altars of colour and texture, and create rituals for the sake of beauty.
Not because it's your business.
Not because it's useful.
Not because anyone will see it.

Because something *inside you* needs to move.
Needs to come alive again.

Creativity is not optional. It's spiritual nutrition.

Feed Your Soul Through Rest

Your body is not a machine.
It is an altar.
And rest is the offering.

Deep, guilt-free rest tells your system: "*I don't have to earn my existence today.*"

This isn't laziness — it's remembrance.
When you rest, you recover parts of yourself that have been lost to survival.
You soften the edges of your being so your soul can land again.
You stop bracing, and you start receiving.

And in rest, the truth has space to rise.

Feed Your Soul Through Connection

Not performance-based connection. Not proximity. Not digital noise.

True connection.
The kind where you're seen *without effort.*
The kind where you stop managing how you're perceived and start simply *being.*

The soul longs to be witnessed in its rawness.
It blooms in honest, messy, heart-led communion.
And this includes connection to others, to the earth, to the body, and to self.

This is why women feel so lost when they're disconnected.
Not because they're broken.
But because the soul cannot thrive in isolation or performance.
It needs *truthful resonance* to stay alive.

You don't need to overhaul your life to feed your soul.
You just need to come back to what's real.
To *what's already calling you home.*

That longing you feel? It's not a problem.
It's not a burden.
It's a sacred summons.

And now you know what to do with it.

Understanding Women

Chapter 12: Where the Ego Belongs

"When the ego runs the show, fear writes the script. When the soul takes the lead, truth becomes the compass."

— **Heather**

The Ego as Gatekeeper, Not Driver

The ego isn't the enemy.
It's not evil. It's not toxic. It's not something to be destroyed.

It's a part of you.
A *necessary* part.
But one that's been given a job it was never designed to do.

The ego was meant to be a gatekeeper — not the driver.

Its role is to protect the system.
To filter. To scan. To pause.
To ask: *"Is this safe?" "Does this serve us?" "Is this aligned?"*

But somewhere along the way, the gatekeeper took the wheel.
And instead of keeping you safe in moments of real danger, it started controlling your life to avoid *perceived* danger.

That's not empowerment.
That's imprisonment dressed up as protection.

When the ego leads, everything becomes about control:

- You don't speak your truth — you manage perceptions.

Understanding Women

- You don't rest — you perform productivity.
- You don't love freely — you calculate risk.
- You don't feel — you analyse.
- You don't create — you perfect.
- You don't grow — you loop.

And most women don't realise it's happening — because ego leadership often *looks* like strength.
But it *feels* like tightness.
Tension. Pressure. Exhaustion.
A life that's full — but never fulfilling.

Here's the truth:

The ego is *brilliant* at protection.
It's just *terrible* at joy.
It doesn't know how to play.
It doesn't know how to rest.
It doesn't know how to be in relationship with the unknown.
And the feminine — *your feminine* — lives in the unknown.

So when the ego leads, the feminine disappears.
And when the feminine disappears, the soul starves.
And when the soul starves, we start to mistake fear for wisdom and armour for power.

You don't need to silence your ego.
You just need to reassign its role.

Say to it: "*Thank you for trying to keep me safe. Now sit in the passenger seat. I'm driving now. And the road ahead doesn't require fear — it requires presence.*"

Because the truth is, the ego can help guide your life — but only when it's reporting to something deeper than itself.

And that "something" is the soul.

Understanding Women

How Ego Hijacks Both Masculine and Feminine Energies

When the ego goes unchecked, it doesn't just lead the system — it *hijacks* the energies meant to serve your wholeness.

It takes what is sacred and twists it into strategy.
It takes what is intuitive, and turns it into impulse.
It takes what is powerful, and distorts it into control.

This is how ego hijacks both masculine energy and feminine energy — and makes them work *against* each other instead of *for* the soul.

Ego in the Masculine Energy

Healthy masculine energy is clarity, containment, structure, and aligned action. It protects the feminine. It holds space for feeling. It creates safety through boundaries and focus.

But when hijacked by ego, masculine energy turns into:

- Domination
- Control
- Over-analysis
- Suppression of emotion
- Needing to be right
- Disconnection from intuition
- Hyper-productivity at the expense of presence

This creates a cold, rigid container — where nothing can grow except performance and pressure. It silences the feminine and cuts off the body from its own wisdom.

Ego in the Feminine Energy

Healthy feminine energy is flow, intuition, expression, compassion, and creation. It feels deeply, speaks honestly, moves with soul, and opens to connection.

Understanding Women

But when hijacked by ego, feminine energy turns into:

- Victimhood
- Manipulation
- Over-emotionality used to control others
- Insecurity dressed as intuition
- Entitlement to be understood without self-understanding
- Drama instead of depth
- Codependency disguised as care

This creates chaos.
An emotional storm with no centre.
And it becomes draining — not just for others, but for the woman herself.

When either energy is run by ego instead of soul, it loses its purpose.
Instead of co-existing, the masculine and feminine fight each other internally.
Instead of collaboration, there's competition.
Instead of balance, there's burnout.

The result?
A woman who feels both exhausted and empty.
Overstimulated but undernourished.
Productive but unfulfilled.
Seen but not known.
Busy but lost.

You don't need to shut down your masculine or suppress your feminine.
You just need to remove ego from their command post.

Because these energies aren't the problem.
The ego's misuse of them is.

Understanding Women

Training the Ego to Serve the Soul, Not Silence It

You don't need to kill the ego.
You need to train it.

The ego isn't bad — it's just over-promoted.
It's been left in charge of things that were never its job — your relationships, your creativity, your truth, your voice, your joy.

The soul is meant to lead.
But the soul is soft-spoken.
It doesn't push. It doesn't perform. It doesn't punish.

So if you've spent a lifetime listening to the loudest voice in your head, it's no wonder the ego took over.

It simply stepped in because no one else was allowed to.

Training the ego begins with awareness.

Start noticing:

- When your thoughts come from fear, not truth
- When your reaction is rooted in defence, not alignment
- When your boundaries are actually walls
- When your achievements are attempts to prove your worth
- When your silence is actually self-abandonment

Every time you recognise an ego pattern, you create the opportunity to shift it.

That's the training. And then? You reassign the ego. You give it a job it's *actually good at:*

- Discernment
- Alertness
- Filtering who and what belongs in your space

- Helping you say "no" with clarity
- Protecting the sacredness of your inner world
- Noticing red flags *without* making them your identity

Let it become the gatekeeper again — not to control your soul, but to protect the space it needs to thrive.

Here's a simple practice:

When you feel ego rise — panic, performance, urgency, the need to be right — pause and say inwardly: *"This is not the soul speaking. I thank you, ego, for your protection. But I choose to lead from trust now."*

The ego won't vanish. But it will *respond to being seen and reassigned.* It will calm when it knows it's not being abandoned — but also not being allowed to drive anymore.

This is not about shaming your ego.
It's about growing up your inner leadership system.

Because the most powerful women are not the ones who fight their ego.
They're the ones who *train it* to stand down in the presence of truth.

Repositioning Inner Authority with Compassionate Discipline

Reclaiming your life from the ego doesn't mean getting harsh.
It means becoming clear.
Consistent.
Kind.
And lovingly unwilling to let fear keep running the show.

This is what true inner authority looks like.
Not dominance. Not rigidity. Not endless self-correction.

It looks like compassionate discipline.
The kind that says:

- *"I know you're scared. But we're not making choices from fear anymore."*
- *"I know this is familiar. But we're here to grow, not repeat."*
- *"I love you. But I won't abandon the truth just to stay comfortable."*

Compassionate discipline is the sacred art of keeping your energy clean.

It's holding boundaries *with yourself* before anyone else needs to. It's recognising when you're avoiding, bypassing, collapsing, or controlling — and choosing to *pause, breathe,* and *redirect.*

It's saying:

- *"I see the pattern. I choose the presence."*
- *"I hear the fear. I choose the truth."*

This is the inner reparenting most of us were never taught.
Not punishment.
Not indulgence.
Just the deep, consistent holding of your own *maturity.*

You are not your ego. You are the one who *sees it.*
You are not the pattern. You are the one with the power to *pause* it.
You are not the reaction. You are the one who can *rewrite* it.

And that's the true gift of compassionate discipline: It doesn't crush the ego. It *relieves* it — from the job it was never supposed to carry.

You lead now.
With clarity.
With care.
With a self-respect so grounded that your ego finally gets to rest — and your soul gets to rise.

Part Five: The Inner Intelligence of Women

Understanding Women

Chapter 13: The Intelligence of the Female Body

"Your body isn't a problem to fix. It's a truth to feel, a home to return to, and a map that already knows the way."

— Heather

The Body as a Living Map of Inner Truth

Your body is not just a vehicle.
It is a living map — an intelligent, emotional, intuitive system that holds every truth your mind has forgotten.

The body remembers.
It remembers who you were before the masks.
Before the roles.
Before the pressure to be palatable, productive, perfect.

It remembers every moment you felt silenced.
Every time you braced instead of breathed.
Every "yes" that should have been a "no."
Every emotion that had nowhere to go.
Every longing that got buried in performance.

And it holds all of that — not to punish you, but to guide you home.

We live in a culture that teaches us to leave the body:

- To override hunger, exhaustion, intuition
- To treat emotions as inconveniences
- To see cycles as problems

- To numb pain and avoid pleasure
- To analyse ourselves instead of feel ourselves

But when you live outside your body, you live outside your truth. You can't feel what's real. You can't sense what you need. You can't hear what your life is asking of you.

You become disembodied — present in theory, but not in practice. And the more disembodied you are, the easier it becomes to betray yourself without even noticing.

Here's the truth: Your body is the most accurate truth-teller you'll ever meet.
It knows when you're aligned.
It knows when you're pretending.
It knows when you're performing instead of feeling.
It knows when you've abandoned yourself to keep the peace, to keep the love, to keep it all together.

And it will always — *always* — let you know.
Through tension.
Through fatigue.
Through resistance.
Through desire.
Through pain.
Through longing.
Through the quiet ache that says: "*This isn't it.*"

Coming home to your body isn't about fixing it.
It's about re-inhabiting it.
Noticing it.
Listening to it.
Trusting that it holds wisdom your mind can't reach.

Because the truth isn't "out there."
It's *in here*.
And your body is the map that shows you the way.

Understanding Women

Listening to the Body's Signals, Pain, and Pleasure

Your body is not a mystery to be solved.
Nor is it a lump of matter that needs to be fixed.
It is a living system, home to a profoundly intelligent, intricate, and emotional map.

Every sensation, every symptom, every reaction — it's all information.

But most women were taught to ignore the signals.
To override the pain.
To perform through the exhaustion.
To mistrust the pleasure.
To silence the sensitivity.
To treat the body as something separate from the self — as something to manage, rather than understand.

So the body keeps speaking.
Louder.
And louder.
Until the whisper becomes a scream.

Pain is not random.
It is the body's language of unmet need.

- A tight chest might say: "*You're not breathing. You're bracing.*"
- A sore throat might whisper: "*There's something you're not saying.*"
- Chronic fatigue might plead: "*Please stop pretending you're fine.*"
- Headaches might signal: "*Your mind is carrying too much, too fast.*"
- Gut tension might cry: "*You don't feel safe.*"

These signals aren't betrayals.
They're messages.
They are your system's way of guiding you back into balance.

Understanding Women

But most women respond to the body the way the world does:
With shame.
With frustration.
With disconnection.

Now let's talk about pleasure.
Because here lies another betrayal.

Pleasure, in its purest form, is presence.
It's the body's way of saying:
"Yes. This feels nourishing. This feels safe. This feels alive."

But for many women, pleasure has been poisoned by programming.
We've been taught that pleasure is indulgent.
That softness is laziness.
That joy must be earned.
That rest is weakness.
That sensuality is dangerous, shameful, or only acceptable when someone else benefits from it.

So we stop listening to what feels good.
And we start choosing what *looks* good.
Until our lives become performative — and our bodies become numb.

Pain and pleasure are not opposites.
They are pathways.

They lead you to what is true.
They reveal what your mind isn't yet ready to say.
They point to the places you've abandoned, denied, suppressed, or forgotten.

And the invitation is this:
To stop outsourcing your truth.

To stop overriding your body's knowing.
To say with deep inner authority:

- *"I feel this."*
- *"I honour this."*
- *"I trust this."*

Because when you begin listening to your body with reverence — not resistance — everything begins to shift.

The tension softens.
The nervous system recalibrates.
The inner world starts to speak more clearly.
And the self you've been longing for… finally feels safe enough to come home.

Understanding Hormonal, Emotional, and Intuitive Feedback

Your body is not a random collection of organs and systems. It's a finely attuned, multidimensional feedback loop — one that speaks through hormones, emotions, and intuition, all at once.

But if no one ever taught you how to listen, those signals can feel like chaos.

Mood swings.
Energy crashes.
Waves of sadness or rage.
Gut reactions you can't explain.

You might think you're broken. You're not. You're just untrained in your own brilliance.

Hormonal Feedback

Hormones are not just about fertility or cycles. They are chemical messengers of your internal truth.

Understanding Women

They respond to:

- Stress
- Sleep
- Food
- Thoughts
- Environment
- Boundaries
- Beliefs

Every time you override your needs...
Every time you people-please, suppress, or push through...
Your hormones adjust to match that reality.

And over time, they send you messages:

- *"I'm tired."*
- *"I'm inflamed."*
- *"I don't feel safe."*

Hormonal imbalance isn't just a medical issue.
It's often a messenger — a sign that your life is out of alignment.

Emotional Feedback

Emotions are not irrational.
They are intelligent responses to your inner and outer world.

Each one carries a message:

- Anger: *A boundary has been crossed.*
- Sadness: *Something needs grieving.*
- Anxiety: *There's a fear here that needs safety, not fixing.*
- Joy: *This is your soul saying yes.*

But most women are only taught to be “pleasant.”
To suppress the emotions that don’t make others comfortable.
To apologise for intensity.
To feel shame for feeling deeply.

So we stop trusting our emotions. And when we stop trusting our emotions, we lose access to the part of ourselves that knows what is true.

Intuitive Feedback

Then there’s intuition — often the most silenced of all.

You’ve felt it:
That knowing in your gut.
That inner yes or no before logic even speaks.
That subtle pull toward something — or away.

But when you’ve been trained to doubt your body, your emotions, and your own voice, intuition gets filed under *unreliable* or *irrational*.

In reality, it’s the purest form of feedback your body can offer.
It’s not based on fear.
It’s not reactive.
It’s ancient, grounded, wise — and always present.

It doesn’t scream.
It doesn’t convince.
It *knows*.

When you begin to honour all three layers — hormonal, emotional, and intuitive — your body becomes a compass, not a burden.

You stop needing external validation.
You stop feeling confused about your needs.

You start moving through life with the kind of calm clarity that only comes from being in relationship with your own system.

Because your body has been trying to speak to you all along.
It's not too late to start listening.

Coming Home to Your Physical Presence

Coming home to your body is not about looking a certain way.
It's not about achieving peak health or perfect balance.
It's about presence.
It's about belonging to yourself, right here, right now.

Because most women have been conditioned to live everywhere *but* in their bodies.

We live in our heads — spinning, analysing, planning, doubting.
We live in other people's needs.
We live in performance, projection, perfectionism.
We live for the approval we might earn — someday, somehow.

But we do not live inside ourselves.
And this disconnection is the root of so much suffering.

Your body is your first home.
Your truest home.
And it has been waiting for you to come back.

Not to take control.
Not to fix or improve.
But simply to *be with* — to witness, to honour, to feel.

Because when you are present in your body:

- Your nervous system begins to settle.
- Your decisions become clearer.

- Your emotions feel safe to rise and move.
- Your intuition gets louder.
- Your pain has space to soften.
- Your pleasure has space to bloom.

You begin to feel whole again — not because your life is perfect, but because *you are finally here.*

Coming home to your physical presence means slowing down enough to feel what's real.
It means not rushing past the signals.
Not bypassing the discomfort.
Not needing to justify your rest, your no, your longing, your yes.

It means saying: "*I live here now. I trust this vessel. I honour this place. I belong in this skin.*"

Because you do.
You always did.
And your body has never once stopped believing that you would return.

Chapter 14: Awakening the Clair Senses Within

"Psychic senses are not magical or "woo-woo". They're practical. They're real. They are inside everybody. And the sooner you stop ignoring them, the sooner your life starts making sense."

— **Heather**

The Eight Clair Senses and Their Roles

Intuition is not one thing.
It is a language — spoken through the body, soul, and energy field.

It doesn't just whisper through the gut. It flows through eight distinct channels — each one designed to deliver information that doesn't come from logic or traditional perception, but from the subtle, unseen realm.

These aren't mystical gifts reserved for a select few. They are human senses, just as real as sight or sound — only quieter. And most women were never taught how to trust them.

But they've been with you all along.
Waiting to be remembered.

Clairsalience – A Clear Sense of Smell

This is the psychic sense of scent. You might catch a whiff of your grandmother's perfume when no one else is around. You might smell flowers, smoke, salt, or tobacco in a space where it makes no logical sense.

Clairsalience is the body's way of tuning into energy through smell. It's ancient, often overlooked, and deeply connected to memory, spirit, and emotional recall.

Clairgustance – A Clear Sense of Taste

This is the ability to receive energetic or spiritual information through taste.

You might suddenly taste metal, sugar, chocolate, or wine — even without eating. It can be symbolic, or it may link you directly to spirit, memory, or a psychic download.

It's often a confirmation sense, offering intuitive emphasis through flavour.

Clairvoyance – A Clear Sense of Vision

This is the psychic sense most people recognise: inner vision.

You may see symbols, colours, faces, landscapes, or entire scenes play out in your mind's eye. Sometimes it comes in dreams. Other times, it's a flash while you're fully awake.

Clairvoyance is your body's *visual* intuitive channel. It speaks in imagery, metaphor, and motion — offering you glimpses of past, present, and possible futures.

Clairaudience – A Clear Sense of Hearing

This is the intuitive sense of sound.

You might hear your name, a word, a phrase, a piece of advice, or a lyric that speaks directly to your situation. You may hear it in your own voice, or one that's distinct.

It can sound internal, like a thought with more weight — or external, like someone speaking softly beside you. This is how you hear energy and receive spiritual or intuitive messages through tone, language, or resonance.

Clairsentience – A Clear Sense of Gut Feeling

This is your gut. Your body's primal "yes" or "no." You feel it in your belly, your skin, your spine. It shows up as tingling, heaviness, nausea, lightness, or even a wave of warmth or chill. You might feel suddenly uneasy in someone's presence — or deeply safe without knowing why.

Clairsentience is the instinctive, gut-level sense of energetic truth. It is often the first intuitive hit — and the one women are most often taught to ignore.

Claircognizance – A Clear Sense of Knowing

You just know. There's no evidence, no reason — but the knowing is undeniable. It might arrive as a sudden insight, a flash of certainty, or a direct download of truth. You may even find yourself saying things you didn't "think" — you just *knew*.

This is the dominant clair for many highly intuitive leaders, strategists, creatives, and guides. It bypasses logic and plugs you straight into deep inner intelligence.

Clairempathy – A Clear Sense of Emotional Feeling

You don't just observe someone's emotion — you *feel* it. You might pick up sadness in your own chest that doesn't belong to you. Or joy, grief, overwhelm, or anger that enters your emotional field without explanation.

This is not weakness. It's psychic attunement through the heart. Clairempathy allows you to feel the emotional energy of others — often before they speak it themselves.

Clairtangency – A Clear Sense of Touch

This is the ability to perceive energy through physical or energetic contact. You might feel tingling, pressure, warmth, or activation in your hands — or anywhere in the body — when connecting to someone or something. Even remotely.

It goes far beyond psychometry. Clairtangency is the channel through which many healers and energy intuitives *feel* others' energy in their own body. It's the sense that lets you read, track, and respond to the unseen through touch.

You don't have to force any of these open. They're already within you. You just need to notice them, trust them, and stop dismissing what you feel as "just in your head."

Understanding Women

These are not extras.
They are part of your original operating system.
They don't make you magical — they make you whole.

Why Women Are Naturally Intuitive but Often Blocked

Women are born intuitive.
Not because they're more "spiritual," but because they're more tuned in.

The female body is biologically and energetically designed to sense.
To track subtle changes.
To feel what's unspoken.
To receive feedback through emotion, sensation, and energetic presence.

It's not a coincidence that women can feel when a child is unwell before symptoms show. That they can pick up on shifts in tone, mood, or truth in a single breath. That they often *know* something's off — before there's any evidence to prove it.

This isn't superstition.
It's pattern recognition, nervous system responsiveness, and energetic literacy.

But even though women are born deeply intuitive — most are taught to block it.

Here's how it happens:

- You were told you were "too sensitive."
- You were punished for crying or expressing emotion.
- You were told to "stop being dramatic" when your body tried to speak.
- You were taught to obey authority over instinct.
- You were praised for logic and shamed for feeling.
- You were taught to defer, suppress, and perform — not to trust your knowing.

So instead of listening inward, you learned to look outward.
To doubt the nudge.

To silence the whisper.
To apologise for the truth that rose inside you.

And over time, the intuitive system began to close down — not because it was broken, but because it wasn't safe to keep it open.

Intuition thrives in safety.

It doesn't scream.
It doesn't fight.
It doesn't force.

It speaks in quiet clarity.
It waits for stillness.
It softens you into truth.

So if you've been living in constant fight-or-flight...
If you've been performing, protecting, proving...
If you've been stuck in your head for years...

You haven't lost your intuition.
You've just forgotten how to feel safe enough to hear it.

You don't need to *become* intuitive.
You already are.

You just need to:

- Create a space where your nervous system can soften
- Learn to trust your first knowing
- Stop outsourcing truth to logic
- Stop apologising for what you feel
- Stop waiting for the world to approve what your body already knows

Understanding Women

This is not about becoming magical.
It's about becoming whole again.

Because when a woman returns to her intuitive centre, she becomes impossible to manipulate, derail, or suppress.

She is guided by a force that no one else needs to understand — because she knows what is true within herself.

The Role of Trauma in Psychic Sensitivity

There's a reason so many intuitive women feel overwhelmed.
Why their nervous systems are frayed.
Why they feel everything, all the time, and can't seem to switch it off.

It's not just because they're sensitive.
It's because they're sensitive in a world that has never felt safe.

And when you combine deep intuitive ability with unprocessed trauma, you don't just get clarity — you get chaos.

Let's be clear:

Psychic sensitivity is not trauma.
But trauma can amplify or distort the senses.

When a nervous system is dysregulated from chronic stress, suppression, or pain, your intuitive channels get flooded:

- Clairsentience becomes anxiety.
- Clairempathy becomes emotional overwhelm.
- Clairaudience turns into mental noise.
- Claircognizance short-circuits into doubt.

Understanding Women

Your gifts don't vanish.
They just become difficult to discern amidst the noise of a system stuck in survival.

Trauma can do two things to the clair senses:

1. It can shut them down.
   You stop feeling, sensing, knowing — because it's safer not to.

2. It can blow them wide open.
   You feel *everything* — but you can't tell what's yours and what's not.

Both are protective.
Both are understandable.
And neither is your fault.

But healing means learning to re-regulate your system — so your intuition isn't distorted by past pain. The most intuitive women are often the ones who've experienced the most wounding. Not because pain makes you psychic — but because surviving pain forces you to listen deeper, track harder, sense faster. And that's a gift — until it becomes your only way of being.

You are not here to be a trauma-tuned radar for everyone else's pain.

You are here to listen to your own knowing first.
To come back into your body.
To create safety on the inside — so your intuition doesn't have to scream to be heard.

Healing trauma doesn't turn your intuition off.
It just clears the interference.
So your guidance system becomes clean, precise, and trustworthy again.

This is how you move from being hijacked by your gifts — to being held by them.

Practices to Awaken and Trust Your Inner Perception

You don't need to go searching for your intuition.
You need to create the conditions where it can rise.

Intuition doesn't respond to force.
It's not accessed by control, or by striving to "get it right."
It flows through presence, permission, and practice.

The more you honour your energy, the clearer your intuitive channels become.
The more you listen to your first instinct, the stronger your knowing gets.
The more you respond to what feels true — even in small ways — the more your system learns: "*I can trust myself again.*"

Here are some gentle yet powerful practices to help you begin:

Start with One Sense

Don't try to awaken all eight Clairs at once.
Begin with the one that feels most familiar:

- Gut feelings (clairsentience)?
- Knowing things without proof (claircognizance)?
- Seeing images or symbols (clairvoyance)?
- Feeling others' emotions (clairempathy)?

Focus there.
Track it for a week.
Note what comes up.
Ask questions like:

- *"What did I feel before I knew?"*
- *"What did I sense before I acted?"*
- *"Did that first instinct turn out to be right?"*

Understanding Women

You're not forcing anything. You're building relationship.

Practice Gentle Observation

Sit in silence for 3–5 minutes each day.

Drop your attention into the body and notice:

- What sensations are present?
- What emotions are rising?
- What images, words, or knowings come up?
- Do you feel pulled toward or away from anything?

Let your body speak without interruption.
No analysis. No fixing.
Just *witness* what's moving through you.

Ask for Inner Confirmation

When something arises intuitively, ask for a clear, loving confirmation.

Not a test. Not proof.
But a gentle way of affirming the language your intuition is using with you.

Examples:

- "If this is true, let me feel it drop into my belly with calm."
- "If I need to act, show me through clarity, not urgency."
- "If this is alignment, let it feel like a yes in my whole body."

This teaches your system that guidance is safe, not stressful.

Clear Energy Before Receiving

If your energy field is cluttered with other people's emotions, opinions, or projections, your Clair senses will be muffled or hijacked.

Understanding Women

Try this simple clearing visualisation before tuning in:

- *"I release what is not mine."*
- *"I call my energy back to centre."*
- *"I create space for my truth to speak."*

Even just placing your hands on your heart or belly as you say this helps reconnect you to your own field.

Practice Active Listening

Your intuition isn't just about what you feel — it's about how deeply you can listen.

When someone is speaking:

- Turn off your ego transmitter — the inner voice that's trying to rehearse your next response.
- Let go of trying to be helpful, wise, clever, or right.
- Be with them fully — not just with your ears, but with your body.

Ask yourself: *"Can I stay present to the full energy of this moment?"*

This trains your nervous system to become a receptive field — not a broadcasting one. It also clears static from your intuitive channels so you can hear, feel, and receive more accurately.

Play Mind Movies

When someone shares a story or speaks from the heart, allow images to arise. Let your intuitive system show you the *feeling* behind their words. This is clairvoyance, clairsentience, and clairempathy working together — helping you perceive the deeper truth, not just the spoken one.

You might see colours, symbols, moments from their life, or emotional scenes unfolding. Don't grasp for meaning.

Just stay curious.
This builds your visual-intuitive channel with softness and skill.

Respond with Aligned Action

When you feel something strongly — *follow it.*
When you know something's off — *honour it.*
When your system says yes — *lean in.*

Each time you act on intuitive truth, you build self-trust. And self-trust is what brings your intuition from background whisper to guiding compass.

You are already intuitive.
You were born with it.
You've just been taught to override, doubt, or abandon what you know.

But your senses are waiting.
And when you honour them, they don't just guide you — they transform you.

Not into someone new...
But into the woman who finally trusts what she already is.

Understanding Women

Chapter 15: Energy Awareness and the Field We Live In

"Your energy field is not a concept — it's how your body speaks before your words ever form. Everything you think, feel, and believe becomes the atmosphere around you. The moment you start noticing it — you take your power back."

— **Heather**

Your Aura and Subtle Body Intelligence

You are not just a body.
You are an energy field — living, breathing, changing, responding.
Long before you speak, your energy walks into the room.
And long after you leave, your energy often lingers behind.

We all know this on some level.
You've felt it when someone enters the space and instantly shifts the atmosphere.
You've sensed it when someone's smile didn't match their energy.
You've walked into rooms that felt "off" without any visible reason.
That's not imagination.
That's your subtle body intelligence.

Every human has an aura — a field of electromagnetic energy that surrounds and interpenetrates the body.
It's not fluff.
It's not a fantasy.
It's measurable
It's responsive, and extremely real.

Understanding Women

Your aura:

- Expands when you feel safe, connected, creative.
- Contracts when you feel threatened, ashamed, judged.
- Fragments when you're scattered, exhausted, or overwhelmed.
- Becomes dense or heavy when you carry emotions that don't belong to you.

The aura isn't just a bubble of light. It's an *extension of your nervous system* and your energetic boundaries. It's how your body protects you, communicates with the world, and processes unseen information.

Within this field live layers of energetic intelligence:

- The emotional body, which stores feelings and unresolved wounds.
- The mental body, shaped by your beliefs and thought patterns.
- The spiritual body, connected to soul truth, purpose, and guidance.
- The physical layer, which reflects the state of the body and vitality.

When aligned, these layers communicate with each other clearly. You feel grounded. Clear. Intuitive. Whole. When out of sync, the energy field can become cloudy, leaky, or hyper-reactive — leaving you tired, confused, emotionally hijacked, or overwhelmed without obvious cause. Understanding your subtle body is not about becoming more spiritual. It's about becoming more self-aware.

Because if you don't understand how your energy operates, you'll always be vulnerable to other people's.
You'll absorb what isn't yours.
You'll override what *is* yours.
And you'll keep trying to fix emotional or physical symptoms without ever looking at the energetic cause.

You don't need to control your field. You need to become present to it. To feel where your energy expands or contracts. To notice what opens you and what depletes you. To treat your aura not as decoration — but as a living, protective layer of truth.

Understanding Women

How Thoughts, Beliefs, and Emotions Shape Energy

Your energy doesn't just respond to your environment.
It responds to you.

Every thought you think.
Every belief you carry.
Every emotion you suppress, express, or absorb — all of it shapes the energy field you live in and the energy you send out.

We are taught to think of thoughts and emotions as private, internal.
But nothing about them is contained.
They radiate.

They become part of your signal.
They teach people how to engage with you.
They either reinforce your boundaries or leak through them.

Thoughts are not neutral. They're creative.

Every thought generates a frequency.
A single sentence repeated often enough becomes an energetic imprint.

- *"I'm not good enough."*
- *"People always leave me."*
- *"I can't trust anyone."*
- *"If I don't do it all, I'll be abandoned."*

These aren't just ideas.
They're energetic programs.
They start to bend your field around them — creating distortion, depletion, disconnection.

And the body will adapt to those patterns — through posture, tone, hormonal response, fatigue, or illness — until it's rebalanced.

Understanding Women

Beliefs are energy scripts.

They write the script for how your life plays out energetically.

If your core belief is "*I must prove myself to be loved,*" your energy will constantly be in performance mode. It will feel tense, alert, and over-giving. Even if your words say, "I'm fine," your energy will scream, "Please validate me."

You don't need to fix all your beliefs at once. But you *do* need to become aware of what you're carrying — because your aura reflects it back to the world in every interaction.

Emotions move or they stagnate.

Emotion is energy in motion.
When felt and expressed cleanly, emotions move through the field and restore balance.

But when suppressed, they stagnate.
They don't just disappear — they store.
In the joints.
In the gut.
In the heart.
In the aura.

Unfelt grief can form heaviness around the shoulders.
Resentment can settle in the liver field.
Fear can tighten the space around the chest and shrink the aura altogether.

This is not symbolic.
It's energetic biology.

If you want to shift your energy, you must become conscious of what you're putting into it:

- Thought patterns
- Belief systems

- Emotional residues
- Internal narratives
- Self-talk

Your energy is a living record of your inner world.
Not because it's judging you.
But because it's mirroring you.
And that mirror is your greatest teacher.

Understanding Your Personal Field vs. Collective Fields

You don't live in a vacuum.
You are part of a collective field — an energetic atmosphere shared by communities, cultures, workplaces, online spaces, even entire nations.

And just as your personal field is shaped by your thoughts, beliefs, and emotions, the collective field is shaped by the dominant energy of the group.

It's why you can walk into a room and immediately feel the tension — even if no one's said a word.
It's why scrolling social media can leave you feeling depleted or inferior — even if the posts weren't aimed at you.
It's why being around fear-driven people can tighten your chest, and being around creative, grounded people can leave you feeling light and inspired.

These aren't moods.
They're fields.
And they're real.

Your Personal Field:

Your personal field is the energetic space that surrounds you, is inside you, and belongs to you.

It's shaped by:

- Your physical health
- Your emotional state
- Your boundaries
- Your thoughts and beliefs
- Your spiritual practices
- Your current level of presence

When you're centred, rested, clear — you're magnetic.
People feel you.
You hold your own.
You don't get pulled into drama or drained by others.

When you're dysregulated, scattered, overextended — your field becomes porous.
You absorb too much.
You lose your own signal.
You start running other people's energy without even realising it.

Collective Fields:

These are shared energy patterns that can lift you — or trap you.

- A women's group that starts as healing and devolves into venting and blame — collective field distortion.
- A work environment where competition replaces collaboration — collective energetic stress.
- A society where fear, division, and survival are constantly broadcast — mass field trauma.

When you're not aware of the collective field, you can confuse its energy for your own.
You might think *you're* angry, when you're just in an angry space.
You might think *you're* anxious, when you've taken on collective fear.
You might think *you're* broken, when you're just attuned to a system that's deeply out of balance.

You are not immune to collective energy.
But you are not powerless within it.

The key is discernment.

Ask often:

- *"Is this mine?"*
- *"Does this belong to me?"*
- *"What am I picking up on, and do I want to carry it?"*

Learning to tell the difference between your energy and the field around you is not spiritual fluff — it's essential emotional intelligence in a world that is constantly broadcasting noise.

Clearing, Strengthening, and Expanding Your Energetic Presence

Your energy field is not fixed. It's dynamic.
It can be cleared. Strengthened. Expanded. Recalibrated.

But this doesn't happen through wishing or hoping. It happens through intention, awareness, and presence.
Because your energy is not something separate from your life — it *is* your life, in motion.

The more consciously you tend to your field, the more clearly you begin to live.
You stop absorbing everything.
You stop leaking your power.
You stop living from reaction and start living from truth.

Come into Presence, Fully

Your energy stabilises the moment you drop into the now.

Not the future.
Not the past.
Right here. Right now.

Presence is what clears static from your field.
It's what allows you to feel what's real, not just what's familiar.
It's what returns your energy to centre.

Try this:

- *"I am here now"*
- *"I choose to be in my body."*
- *"I choose to feel the truth of this moment."*
- *"Nothing needs to be different. I am safe to be present."*

This isn't spiritual performance.
It's energetic clarity.

And it changes everything.

Stop Comparing Yourself to Anyone

Comparison is an energetic leak.

The instant you compare yourself to someone else, you create imbalance in your field.
You either inflate or diminish — neither of which is truth.

You are not here to be better than anyone.
You are here to become more fully yourself.

The only useful comparison is this:
"Am I more aligned today than I was yesterday?"

Everything else pulls you out of your centre and into someone else's story.
And their story is not your path.

Understanding Women

Stay with your energy.
Refine your own light.
Let others do the same.

Clear Your Energy Daily

Like brushing your teeth or washing your skin, your energy needs clearing.

You can do this in under 2 minutes:

- Visualise: Golden light washing over you, clearing anything that isn't yours.
- Speak: "*I clear what is not mine. I return it with love. I call my energy back to centre.*"
- Ground: Stand barefoot. Breathe deep. Anchor back into your body.

Your field will thank you for the consistency.

Strengthen Through Boundaries and Self-Trust

Energetic boundaries are built through clarity and congruence.

- Say no when your body contracts.
- Say yes when your body opens.
- Don't explain your truth to make others comfortable.
- Don't abandon yourself to be liked.

The more aligned your choices, the stronger your field becomes.

Become an Observer of Your Thoughts

You are not your thoughts.
You are the one *watching* them.

The moment you begin to observe your mind, you stop being ruled by it.
You shine light on the stories, patterns, assumptions — and suddenly, they loosen.

Understanding Women

Watch your inner world like a sky:
Let thoughts pass like clouds.
Let judgments drift without attachment.
Let fear be seen without giving it the microphone.

Presence and observation are what create the gap between reaction and response — and in that gap, your power returns.

Expand Through Alignment and Authenticity

You don't expand by effort. You expand by resonance. You grow when you feel safe to be who you really are.

Ways to expand:

- Speak what's true.
- Move in ways that feel alive.
- Surround yourself with energy that nourishes, not depletes.
- Let your nervous system rest.
- Let your creativity flow.
- Let your soul feel seen.

When you're in alignment, your field expands without trying. You become magnetic — not because you're seeking anything, but because you're being everything you truly are.

Your energetic presence is not an accessory. It's a mirror of your inner world.
You don't need to become more. You just need to become present.
Clear what's not yours. Strengthen what is.

Expand into what wants to come through you. And let your energy speak the truth your voice hasn't yet said: "*I'm here. I'm whole. And I know who I am now.*"

Part Six: Practical Rewiring for a New Womanhood

Understanding Women

Chapter 16: Reaction Reprogramming

“Reaction is the habit of the wounded. Response is the choice of the wise. *You are not here to be ruled by your wounds.*”

— ***Heather***

The Pattern of React-Then-Regret

We all know the moment.

Something gets said.
Or something doesn’t.
A look, a tone, a silence —
And suddenly the body is flooded.
The heart races, the stomach tightens, the mouth opens before the mind has time to arrive.

You react.
And then... you regret.

Not always out loud.
But internally, there’s that quiet shame that whispers:

- *“Why did I say that?”*
- *“Why did I do that?”*
- *“That’s not who I wanted to be.”*

This is the react-then-regret cycle.
And most women are trapped in it without ever realising that there’s a way out.

Understanding Women

What causes the reaction?

It's not just the situation.
It's everything the situation *touches*.

A comment might hit your mother wound.
A tone might echo a past rejection.
An innocent question might land in your nervous system as an attack.

Your reaction isn't about what's happening now.
It's about everything that's ever happened that hasn't been felt, processed, or healed.

It's unprocessed emotion, trapped in the body, *replaying itself in real time.*

This is why "just calm down" never works.
Because when the body is in survival, the mind doesn't get a vote.

The feminine body reacts fast — but heals faster when safe.

Reaction is not failure.
It's a flag.
It's your system saying:
"*Something here needs to be seen.*"

But instead of seeing it, we usually do one of two things:

- Explode: Raise our voice. Use cutting words. Say something we don't mean. Then carry the shame after.
- Implode: Shut down. Go silent. Seethe in resentment. Collapse inward. Then wonder why no one understands us.

Neither of these responses are wrong.
They're survival.
But neither will create the peace we crave.

We don't regret what we felt. We regret how we expressed it.

Understanding Women

You're allowed to feel triggered.
You're allowed to be angry.
You're allowed to have deep, raw emotion.

But there is a difference between having a feeling and being hijacked by it.

Reaction happens when we bypass the feeling and go straight to expression. Healing begins when we pause long enough to feel the emotion first — *fully* — before we speak from it.

This is where the reprogramming begins.

You are not a bad person for reacting.
But you are being invited now to *interrupt* the cycle.

To stop living from the wound.
And start choosing your words from your worth.

Learning to Pause and Feel Before Responding

Pause is power.

Not in the performative, spiritual bypass sense of "just breathe and let it go."
But in the deeply embodied truth of: "*I will not abandon myself in this moment.*"

Because that's what reaction is, really —
A split-second abandonment.
Of your values.
Of your nervous system.
Of your true self.

Reprogramming the pattern doesn't mean never feeling triggered again.
It means learning to hold yourself steady when you are.

The pause is not passive. It's active containment.

Understanding Women

To pause is not to suppress.
It's to make space for the full truth of what's happening inside you.

Your job is not to skip the emotion.
Your job is to meet it.

To say:

- *"I feel the heat of this."*
- *"I notice the old story rising."*
- *"I can feel the charge in my chest, the tightness in my gut."*
- *"But I am still here. I don't have to act from this place."*

That is inner leadership.
That is feminine maturity.

Feel first. Speak later.

When you allow yourself to fully feel what's present — without judgement, without performance — you stop offloading pain and start integrating it.

You begin to notice:

- *"This anger isn't about them. It's about me feeling unseen."*
- *"This sadness is actually old grief that hasn't moved."*
- *"This reaction is trying to protect me — but I no longer need to be protected from this."*

And from there, you can respond — not as the wounded child or the triggered ego — but as the woman you're choosing to become.

The sacred 10-second delay

In any conflict, in any triggering moment, try this: Before you speak — pause for ten seconds. Place your hand on your body. Breathe into the part of you that feels the most activated. Don't analyse. Don't fix. Just feel.

Then ask:

- *"What am I really feeling?"*
- *"Where is this living in my body?"*
- *"What would I say if I weren't afraid of being wrong or misunderstood?"*

This one moment can change everything.

You won't always get it right.
But you will start getting real.

And real is where all the healing begins.

The Power of Language — Replacing Reaction with Expression

Language is a spell.
It either anchors the emotion you're feeling into a deeper wound — or it becomes the bridge that sets you free.

Most reaction happens because we've never been taught how to language emotion. But more importantly — we've never been taught how to correctly identify the emotion in the first place.

We think we're expressing sadness, but we're shouting.
We say we feel "hurt," but it's actually shame.
We claim we're "angry," but underneath is deep grief.

If you misidentify the emotion, you miscommunicate the truth. And when emotion pours out in language without regulation, it stops being expression — and starts being emotional aggression.

We jump from feeling straight to defence.
From discomfort straight to blame.
From vulnerability straight to shutdown or explosion.
But there's a different path.

Understanding Women

It's called expression — and it begins with emotional fluency.
And that fluency begins with emotional precision.

Real expression doesn't come from needing to be right.

It comes from recognising what's true — beneath the reactivity, the story, the justification.

If you say: "*I feel deeply saddened*" while raising your voice and slamming doors — that's not felt sadness. That's unprocessed rage in disguise.

If you say: "*I just feel really hurt*" while blaming or accusing — you're not expressing hurt. You're projecting pain.

The body can feel the difference.
So can everyone around you.

The ego wants to be right. The soul wants to be real.

Most reactive communication is ego-driven:

- "*You always...*"
- "*You never...*"
- "*How dare you...*"
- "*I can't believe you would...*"

These are defence mechanisms, not truth.

But when you return to the body — when you pause, feel, and express without attack — you give the other person space to actually hear you, instead of defending themselves from you.

This is how conflict becomes connection.
This is how reaction becomes repair.
This is how you speak like a woman who knows herself.

Replace reactivity with clarity.

If you're someone who tends to lash out, try this:

- Write down what you want to say, unfiltered.
- Let it all out onto the page.
- Then sit with it. Breathe with it.
- Ask: *"What's the truth behind this emotion?"*
- Highlight one or two clear sentences that express what you actually need to be heard.
- Speak from there.

Here's the correction: Feel fully. Then speak cleanly.

Before you say a word, ask yourself:

- *"What am I actually feeling?"*
- *"Where is it landing in my body?"*
- *"Am I speaking this to be seen — or to punish?"*

Expression without this inner check is still reactivity — dressed up in nicer language.

But when you feel fully — without needing to react — you access a level of clarity that doesn't require volume, drama, or defence.

Clean expression sounds like this:

- *"I notice I'm feeling shame, and I want to run. But I'm here."*
- *"I feel rejected, and I can see this has touched something old in me."*
- *"I feel grief, and I don't need it to be fixed. I just need to say it out loud."*
- *"I'm feeling overwhelmed, and I want to speak from clarity, not reaction. Can we take a pause?"*
- *"When that happened, I felt dismissed. I know that might not have been your intent, but that's how it landed in my body."*
- *"This brought up something old for me, and I'd like to share it when I'm grounded."*
- *"I'm not trying to win this — I'm trying to be honest about what I'm feeling."*

Understanding Women

This isn't softness for the sake of being nice.
It's strength rooted in self-awareness.
It's the difference between unloading your emotion and owning it.

This is emotional maturity.
This is self-leadership.
This is the difference between emotional honesty and emotional dumping.

Truth needs no volume.

The clearer your language, the quieter you can be.
Because when the feeling is owned — and cleanly named — there's no need to shout it over the top of your own dysregulation.

This is not about silencing your fire.
It's about choosing when and how to light the flame.

You don't lose your power by pausing.
You gain it — because you're no longer giving your energy away to unconscious patterns.

This is what real self-expression sounds like:
Rooted. Clear. Felt.
Not defensive. Not chaotic. Not a performance.

Real expression happens when the emotion has already been felt inside you.
Then your words don't come from pain — they come from peace.
And people feel the difference immediately.

This is how we stop using emotion as a weapon and start using it as the language of connection.

Practice – Journaling and Feeling Before Speaking

If you want to change your patterns, you have to change where you begin.

Most people move through life on autopilot:
Situation → Reaction → Behaviour → Feeling.

Something happens.
They react — unconsciously, habitually.
They behave based on that reaction.
Only afterward do they feel the consequences — usually regret, shame, anger, sadness.

This is not because they're bad.
It's because they're untrained.

You were never taught to insert consciousness between the stimulus and the response.

You were never shown how to *feel* first, *choose* second, *act* third.

But you can retrain yourself.
You can shift the sequence to:
Situation → Feeling → Reaction → Behaviour.

This seems small on paper.
It's transformational in real life.

The Old Pattern:

Situation (someone criticises you) →
Reaction (you snap back defensively) →
Behaviour (you say something you later regret) →
Feeling (shame, resentment, guilt).

The New Pattern:

Situation (someone criticises you) →
Feeling (*Pause.* "I feel hurt. I feel defensive.") →

Reaction (*Pause longer.* "I choose to breathe instead of defend.") →
Behaviour (you express, "That comment stung. Can we talk about it without blame?").

How to Practice This Through Journaling:

1. Replay a situation where you reacted. Write it down in raw detail — what happened, what you felt, what you did.
2. Identify the first body feeling. Was it a clenching? A heat rising? A contraction? Before you spoke, where did you feel it?
3. Notice your automatic reaction. What did you do immediately? Lash out? Withdraw? Blame? Defend?
4. Ask yourself:
    - "*What was I really feeling?*"
    - "*What belief got triggered?* "(e.g., "I'm not good enough," "I don't matter.")
    - "*What did I actually need in that moment?*" (Safety, validation, space?)
5. Rewrite the scene. Imagine inserting the conscious pause. Imagine feeling the feeling *before* reacting. Choose a new response. Write it out.

The Shift Happens When You Slow It Down.

At first, it won't happen in real time. You'll journal after the fact. You'll reflect after the blow-up or the shutdown. But over time, with enough conscious review, your system will start recognising the signs sooner.

You'll start feeling the feeling before the reaction ignites.
You'll catch yourself mid-pattern.
And eventually — you'll pause in real life, not just on the page.

This practice isn't about perfection. It's about presence. It's about becoming the woman who can stand inside a wave of emotion and still choose truth over drama, connection over control, peace over performance.

The old cycle was never your fault.
But the new cycle —
That's your power now.

Chapter 17: Boundaries: The Masculine Role in a Feminine Life

"Every time you overstep into someone else's life, you abandon your own. Containment is where true compassion begins."

— ***Heather***

The Feminine Must Be Protected to Thrive

The feminine energy within you is not weak.
It is wild, radiant, creative, nurturing, intuitive, deeply feeling.
But it is also profoundly sensitive to the environment it lives in — both internally and externally.

The feminine cannot thrive without protection.
Not domination.
Not control.
Protection.

And that protection is not something you wait for the world to give you. It is something you must first give yourself — by building a strong internal masculine energy.

This is not about gender.
This is about energy.

It doesn't matter whether you are a woman, a man, or identify outside the binary. Every thriving human being needs both healthy masculine and feminine energies inside them.

Without protection, the feminine collapses.

Understanding Women

When the feminine is not protected — internally or externally — she contracts.
She hardens.
She lashes out.
Or she hides.

She moves into fear instead of flow.
She becomes defensive instead of creative.
She becomes angry instead of open.
She hides herself instead of shining her radiant light.
Not because she is wrong — but because she is exposed.

A flower cannot bloom if the soil is poisoned or the roots are pulled at every turn.
A river cannot run clear if the banks are broken and no container holds its direction.

In the same way, the feminine energy in you needs healthy containment in order to truly live.

Healthy boundaries are an act of internal masculine leadership.

They are not walls of fear.
They are structures of safety.
They are the masculine energy inside you standing tall and saying:

- *"This is how we honour ourselves."*
- *"This is how we protect the space we need to create, to love, to breathe."*
- *"This is what is allowed in. This is what must stay outside."*

Without boundaries, the feminine becomes resentful, brittle, overexposed. She becomes everything she was never meant to be — because she is living without a home inside herself.

Boundaries are not selfish.
They are sacred.

They are what allow the feminine to remain soft without being vulnerable to violation, creative without being depleted, open without being overrun.

Internal safety must come before external safety.

You can build castles of stone.
You can demand that the world treat you better.
You can cut people off and protect yourself endlessly —

But if you do not build a safe place inside your own energy system, the world will only mirror back to you the instability you still carry.

When you embody your healthy internal masculine — your boundaries, your standards, your protection — the world feels it.
And you will naturally attract people, opportunities, and relationships that reflect that back.

You do not command respect by force.
You embody respect by how you care for yourself.

And the feminine inside you?
She will breathe deeper.
She will sing louder.
She will move more freely.

Because she knows — at last — that she is safe.

How to Build Boundaries with Kindness and Strength

Building boundaries is not about becoming rigid, defensive, or aggressive. It's about creating a clear energetic structure that honours both yourself and others.

Boundaries built from fear are walls.
Boundaries built from love are bridges.

Understanding Women

When you create boundaries with kindness and strength, you aren't shutting people out — you're creating clear pathways for how you want to be engaged with. You are protecting the space in which your true self can thrive.

Kindness Without Strength is Fragile. Strength Without Kindness is Hard.

Most women have been trained to believe they must choose one:

- Be endlessly kind and let everyone in.
- Or be fiercely strong and push everyone away.

Neither alone is sustainable.

Kindness without strength becomes self-abandonment.
Strength without kindness becomes isolation.

True boundaries are both:

- Kindness says: *"I see your humanity."*
- Strength says: *"But I choose my well-being first."*

When you build boundaries this way, you are no longer reacting — you are leading. You are no longer trying to control others — you are controlling your own space.

The Essentials of Kind and Strong Boundaries:

Be clear, not cryptic. Say what you mean. Say it simply. Say it early.
"I can't take that call today."
"I need some time to recharge."
"I'm not available for that kind of conversation."

Own your needs without apology. You don't need to justify, defend, or explain yourself into exhaustion. A boundary is valid because it honours your system, not because someone else agrees with it.

Stay grounded, not guilty. Feeling guilty after setting a boundary doesn't mean the boundary was wrong. It means your nervous system is learning something new. Breathe through it.

Use "I" language instead of blame. Speak from your centre, not from accusation.
"I need..." instead of "You always..."
"I feel better when..." instead of "You make me feel..."

Hold the line with love. When the boundary is tested — and it will be — stay steady. You don't have to fight. You don't have to collapse. You simply stand where you already decided to stand.

You teach people how to treat you by how you treat yourself.

Every time you set a boundary with kindness and strength, you reinforce the message: *"This is a sacred space."* You show others how to love you by how you love yourself. You show others how to respect you by how you respect yourself.

And most importantly — you allow the feminine energy inside you to flourish, because she knows she is no longer exposed, no longer overrun, no longer sacrificed.

She is safe.
She is home.
She is free.

Stop Leaking Energy into Other People's Lives

Most women think of boundaries as a way to stop others from draining them.
But here's the truth that very few are ready to hear:

You're not just on the receiving end of energy leaks — you're often the source.

We speak of being overwhelmed, exhausted, and energetically overrun.
But how often are we over-involved in the lives of others?

- Offering advice that wasn't asked for
- Meddling in dynamics that aren't ours to fix
- Scanning social media for clues about exes or friends
- Emotionally babysitting people who haven't chosen their own healing
- Holding onto resentment, stories, or pain that no longer belong to this moment

It's not just others we need to protect ourselves from.
It's our own habits of overgiving, over-attaching, over-involving.

Boundaries Go Both Ways.

Most people want to build boundaries around what comes into their lives. But fewer are willing to build boundaries around what they project out.

Energetic maturity means recognising:

- *"This is not my story to carry."*
- *"I don't need to be involved in how they live their life."*
- *"My opinion is not needed here."*
- *"Their emotions are not mine to manage."*
- *"Their choices are theirs. I choose peace over control."*

We speak of energy protection like we're under constant attack. But sometimes, we're the ones overreaching.

You are not emotionally responsible for anyone else's life.

Not your partner.
Not your parents.
Not your children — outside of true caregiving.
Not your friends, your clients, or your community.

You are responsible to people in your life — for your honesty, your presence, your integrity. But you are not responsible for how they feel, grow, change, or don't. Confusing these two is one of the biggest sources of emotional exhaustion in women.

Energetic Sovereignty Means Knowing Where You End.

This is not disconnection.
This is discernment.

This is being deeply connected, deeply caring — without collapsing into someone else's emotional field.

You don't owe everyone your attention.
You don't have to manage what isn't yours.
You don't have to feel what everyone else is feeling in order to be loving.

Every time you intervene where your presence wasn't requested, you leak energy.
Every time you try to fix someone else's path, you step off your own.

Let your field be clear. Let your presence be sovereign.

When you stop leaking energy outward, you regain the strength to hold your own centre.
You come back into focus.
You come back into you.

You become less reactive.
Less entangled.
Less burned out.

Because the truth is — most of your overwhelm was never yours to carry.

Recognising the Energetic Difference Between Control and Containment?

Let's get honest.

A lot of what we call "holding space," "caring," or "being involved" is actually control in disguise.

It's not loving presence.
It's an unprocessed fear that says:
"If I don't manage this, I'll lose something. If I don't direct this, I'll be abandoned. If I don't interfere, I won't matter."

This is not containment.
It's control.
And it's exhausting for everyone involved.

Control is about others. Containment is about you.

Control says:

- *"Let me help you."* (even when help isn't asked for)
- *"Let me correct you."*
- *"Let me stay involved so I feel needed."*
- *"Let me mother you so I don't have to face my own loneliness."*

Containment says:

- *"I can witness this without trying to fix it."*
- *"I can trust your path, even if it doesn't look like mine."*
- *"I can hold my energy steady without spilling it over you."*
- *"I can let go of needing to be significant in your story."*

Containment is not passive.
It is radical energetic discipline.
It's where the masculine energy inside you becomes a guardian — of your own alignment, and the sacred autonomy of others.

Stop making others accountable for your self-worth.

This might sting, but it's time.

No one is here to validate you.

Understanding Women

No one can fix what you won't face.
The people around you are dealing with their own wounds, their own worth, their own weight.

Stop expecting your partner to fill the cracks in your confidence.
Stop demanding your friends reflect back a version of you that you're not living.
Stop raising children in the image of your unmet needs — then calling it love.

You must know where your story ends and someone else's begins.

Recognise your patterns. Stop repeating them.

Most of what you call "truth" is just repetition.

Repeating the same wound.
The same story.
The same emotional chaos that played out in your family, now playing out in your relationship, your workplace, your self-talk.

And if you don't pause — if you don't bring in structure, discipline, and containment — you will pass that story on.

To your children.
To your partner.
To your community.
To your own nervous system every single day.

You will call it "personality."
You will call it "just how I am."
But it is not.

It is untended pain, seeking a place to land.

You are not here to mother everyone.

And you are certainly not here to smother them.

Understanding Women

Mothering says: "*I see you, and I'll stand beside you.*"
Smothering says: "*I'll wrap myself around your life until I disappear.*"
Disconnection says: "*I'm not responsible for anyone, so I'll shut it all off.*"

None of these bring peace.

Containment is the middle way.
It says:

- "*I will stay centred in myself.*"
- "*I will offer love that does not override.*"
- "*I will honour your journey without projecting mine onto it.*"

This is real maturity.
This is energetic leadership.

Containment is the masculine role in a feminine life.

It is the boundary around your radiance.
The container around your creative flow.
The structure that allows your softness to breathe without collapse.

When you contain your own energy, you stop bleeding into others.
You stop dragging your history into your present.
You stop blaming the past for a future that's still yours to write.

You don't need to be rescued.
You need to be reclaimed.

And that begins the moment you stop confusing control with care — and start standing inside the sacred strength of your own clear centre.

Chapter 18: Stop the Spread of Judgment, Criticism, and Blame

"Your judgments don't define anyone. They define what you haven't met in yourself. You don't clear pain by casting it on others — you clear it by facing it, feeling it, and choosing to grow and then exist beyond it."

— **Heather**

The Mirror — What You Judge Is Yours to Heal

Judging someone doesn't define them.
It defines you.
It says: "*I need to judge in order to make sense of what I don't yet understand.*"

It reveals more about what's unsettled in you than it ever does about them.
Because the truth is — judgment is rarely about the person being judged.
It's about the internal discomfort that gets stirred up in the one doing the judging.

Judgment is not insight.
Criticism is not truth.
And blame is not clarity.

They are all distortions of pain — projected outward, because inward would feel too confronting.

When we judge someone else, what we're often doing is revealing the part of ourselves we're unwilling to meet.
Their choices press on our shame.
Their emotions mirror the ones we've repressed.

Understanding Women

Their power activates our comparison.
Their softness exposes our hardness.

And rather than sit with that discomfort, we attack, analyse, diminish, or dismiss.

Every judgment is a mirror.

- When you judge another woman for being "too much," it may be because you've silenced your own fullness.
- When you criticise someone for being too loud, too sensitive, too confident — it may be the parts of yourself you weren't allowed to express.
- When you feel reactive to someone's softness, success, calm, or chaos — it's almost always a signal.

"*This is something inside me that hasn't found peace.*"

The external world will always reflect what's unintegrated within.
Judgment just shows you where the work is waiting.

You spot it because you've got it.

This isn't about blame.
It's about honesty.

If you didn't carry the frequency somewhere in your own field, it wouldn't trigger you.
It might still be observable — but it wouldn't hook you.
It wouldn't activate that reaction in your nervous system that says, "*That's wrong. That needs to stop. That's not okay.*"

Yes, sometimes you're sensing misalignment or truth.
But often, the sharper the reaction, the more personal the echo.

This is why judgment doesn't bring clarity — it brings confusion.
Because it makes it about *them*, when the healing lives inside *you*.

Judgment keeps you stuck in separation.

Understanding Women

When you're in judgment, you're not in your power.
You're in projection.

And projection is seductive because it feels righteous.

- "They're the problem."
- "That energy is toxic."
- "He's fake."
- "She's a narcissist."
- "They're not on my level."

All of that may feel true in the moment. But when you say it from a place of reaction, superiority, or resentment — you stay in the wound.

You never rise out of it.
You just loop it louder.

What you judge, you strengthen. What you accept, you free.

That's the paradox of the mirror.

When you judge something, you give it more energy.
You embed it deeper into your nervous system.
You reinforce the belief that you're separate from what you're seeing — when in truth, you're being shown a part of your own healing through someone else's expression.

But when you accept the mirror — when you own your piece — you collapse the charge.
You reclaim the power.
You no longer need to stay defended.

You can look at someone else and say:

- ***"I see where this touches me."***
- ***"I see where I still have work to do."***
- ***"I see myself here, and I choose to grow."***

Understanding Women

Why We Attack Others to Avoid Growing Ourselves

Let's say it plainly:
It is easier to attack someone else than to admit you are still hurting.
It is easier to label, dismiss, or lash out than it is to feel your own shame.

That's why most criticism is not strength.
It's self-protection.

We lash out when we feel small.
We become cruel when we feel powerless.
We diminish others when we're afraid we've been diminished ourselves.

And we call it clarity.
We call it confidence.
We call it "just telling it like it is."

But what it really is, is avoidance.

Unowned pain always finds someone to land on.

It doesn't just disappear.
It seeps out.

In passive-aggressive comments.
In gossip.
In cold silences.
In defensiveness.
In self-elevation through someone else's perceived inferiority.
In the inability to celebrate another woman without positioning yourself as better, wiser, more experienced, or more deserving.

You see it in family dynamics all the time:

Understanding Women

- A mother-in-law putting down her daughter-in-law to maintain social or emotional rank in her son's life.
- A wife bigging up her husband's status to position herself as superior to the other women in the room.
- A woman who cannot sit beside another woman's glow without needing to announce her own relevance.

These are all forms of energetic attack — socially accepted, often unspoken, but just as damaging. And they don't come from power. They come from pain.

Attack is not feedback. It's fear.

It's the fear that you're not enough.
The fear that you're falling behind.
The fear that if someone else is shining, it means you won't be seen.
The fear that if someone else is loved, it means there's less for you.

The feminine wound here is deep. Many women are carrying unresolved grief, comparison, jealousy, abandonment, and shame. And instead of feeling it, owning it, healing it — they displace it.

They turn it into judgment.
They weaponise it as criticism.
They mask it as "discernment" or "energy reading."

But the body knows the difference.
So does your field.

Every attack is a request for healing.

When you find yourself triggered by someone's success, beauty, softness, boundaries, voice, confidence — pause and ask:

- *"What part of me feels left behind?"*
- *"What belief is being challenged by their existence?"*

- *"What wound is surfacing underneath this story I'm telling about them?"*
- *"Am I actually seeing them clearly — or just seeing them through my pain?"*

Because real growth does not come from tearing others down. It comes from recognising your own emotional reactions and choosing to rise through them, not fling them outward.

This is radical accountability.
This is spiritual maturity.
This is how women stop wounding one another in the name of their own healing.

Clearing the Internal Critic Without Losing Self-Honesty

There's a fine line between self-awareness and self-abuse.

Most women think they're being honest with themselves when actually, they're being brutal.

The voice in their head says:

- *"You should know better."*
- *"You're not doing enough."*
- *"No one wants to hear you."*
- *"You're too much. You're not enough."*

And they call it truth.
But it's not truth.
It's internalised shame, disguised as accountability.

This voice didn't come from nowhere.
It came from being criticised too young, too often, too unfairly.
It came from emotional environments where praise was scarce and perfection was the standard.
It came from school systems, family systems, religious systems, cultural systems that equated being good with being silent, obedient, thin, nice, or never angry.

Understanding Women

Now, that voice lives in your head.
And you repeat it — on loop.

You cannot love yourself by hating yourself into change.

No amount of criticism will bring peace.
No amount of shame will create confidence.
No amount of inner harshness will lead to genuine self-respect.

All it will do is keep you stuck — performing your life instead of living it.

Because self-attack does not make you grow.
It makes you small.

So how do you clear the inner critic — without losing the power of self-honesty?

You learn to separate truth from tone.

The truth might be:

- *"I wasn't kind today."*
- *"I interrupted her."*
- *"I spoke from fear."*
- *"I was projecting."*

That's accountability.

But if your inner voice follows that with:

- "What's wrong with me?"
- *"I'm such a terrible person."*
- "No wonder *no one stays in my life."*
- That's self-punishment.

The difference is this:
One builds awareness.
The other builds shame.

You are allowed to see what needs healing — without using it as a weapon against yourself.

Real self-honesty is grounded. It's gentle.
It's the voice of the woman who is ready to lead herself through the next layer of growth.
Not with guilt. Not with punishment.
But with precision. With presence. With willingness.

It sounds like:

- *"That was out of alignment. Let's choose differently next time."*
- *"This pattern is coming up again. What am I still avoiding?"*
- *"I didn't speak from my centre. Let me return to it."*
- *"That wasn't who I want to be. I'm still learning — and I will course-correct."*

This is how you clean the mirror without breaking it.
This is how you rise with clarity, not cruelty.

Reprogramming Internal Dialogue for Growth

You cannot live a peaceful life with a voice in your head that speaks to you like an enemy.

You may have outgrown old environments.
You may have cut ties, set boundaries, moved on.
But if the voice inside you still echoes those same patterns of criticism, then the past is still living through your present.

And you cannot grow into the woman you are here to become if you're still narrating your life from an outdated, unkind script.

Your inner voice is not fixed. It's programmable.

Understanding Women

Every thought you think creates a neural pathway.
Every phrase you repeat strengthens a belief.

So if you tell yourself:

- *"I'm too sensitive."*
- *"I never get it right."*
- *"I don't belong."*
- *"I'll never be like her."*

You're not just speaking.
You're wiring your nervous system to expect rejection, unworthiness, and failure.

But the same mechanism that programmed the inner critic is the one that can rewrite it.

Reprogramming starts with consistency, not perfection.

Start small. Speak clearly. Interrupt the narrative.

When the critic rises, meet it with something like:

- *"Thank you, but I don't speak to myself like that anymore."*
- *"That thought isn't mine. That's old conditioning."*
- *"I choose a different voice now — one that helps me grow."*

Then insert the new language, like:

- *"I'm doing better than I think."*
- *"It's safe to speak gently to myself."*
- *"Even in my imperfection, I am worthy of compassion."*
- *"This is hard, but I'm learning."*

You don't need to fake positivity.
You need to choose truth — kindly spoken, clearly held.

You are always teaching your nervous system how safe it is to be you.

Understanding Women

If your inner voice is full of shame, pressure, judgment, or urgency, your body will never feel safe to rest, to soften, or to rise.

But if your voice becomes an ally — one that tells the truth with care, one that calls you forward without dragging you down — then your entire life starts to change.

You begin to attract people who mirror that same energy.
You begin to make decisions that honour your growth.
You begin to live from a space of gentle power.

You are allowed to speak to yourself like someone worth loving.

Because you are.

And the moment you stop using your inner voice as a weapon, and start using it as a guide, you reclaim the part of you that never needed to be fixed — just *finally*, truly heard.

Part Seven: A New Feminine Future

Understanding Women

Chapter 19: Self-Love as Sacred Practice

When self-love leads, life gets cleaner. Not easier — cleaner. Because you stop negotiating your worth. You don't need to believe it right away. You just need to say it — again and again — until your system starts to remember it's true."

— **Heather**

It's Not a Buzzword – It's Brain Rewiring

Self-love has been watered down.

Turned into hashtags and bubble baths.
Brushed over with pastel affirmations and filtered quotes.
Packaged as a luxury, not a necessity.

But real self-love?
It's not trendy.
It's not fluffy.
And it's definitely not optional.

It's brain rewiring.
It's nervous system regulation.
It's the act of turning your own internal environment into a place where you feel safe to exist.

Self-love is not a feeling. It's a practice.

It's what you do when no one is watching.
It's the voice you use when you mess up.

Understanding Women

It's the decision you make when shame knocks at your door, and you say, "*Not today — I know who I am.*"

It's showing up for yourself even when you don't feel worthy of being shown up for. Especially then.

Self-love is built in micro-moments:

- Choosing food that nourishes your body, not just silences your emotion.
- Going to bed instead of scrolling for reassurance.
- Saying no, even when you feel guilty.
- Letting yourself feel, instead of perform.
- Speaking kindly to yourself in the quiet.

These things are not small.
They are rewiring your brain to believe,
"*I am safe. I am held. I am enough.*"

Without self-love, every decision is made from fear.

You stay in the wrong relationship because you don't believe you deserve better.
You silence yourself in rooms that need your voice.
You exhaust yourself proving your worth to people who can't see it.
You abandon yourself to keep peace — until you have no peace at all.

And none of it looks like lack of self-love from the outside.
It looks like being agreeable. Accommodating. Ambitious.
But inside, it feels like constant tension, anxiety, disconnection, resentment.

Because the absence of self-love always shows up as a presence of inner conflict.

You don't build self-love by thinking about it. You build it by choosing it — again and again.

Understanding Women

Every time you make a loving choice in the face of a fear-based habit, you're building a new neural pathway.
A new pattern.
A new possibility.

Self-love is not a destination.

It's not a moment of arrival.

It's a relationship you keep nurturing until the voice inside your head becomes your greatest ally, and the energy inside your body becomes the safest place you know.

5 Minutes a Day to Rebuild Your Neural Pathways to Peace

You don't need a 30-day challenge.
You don't need a spiritual overhaul.
You don't even need to feel like it.

You need five minutes.

Five minutes of focused self-love a day is enough to start rewiring your brain.

This isn't wishful thinking.
It's neuroscience.
Your brain listens to repetition.
Your nervous system listens to tone.
And your sense of safety builds every time you show up for yourself in a new way.

Start with this: 5 minutes of pure self-worth language.

Find a quiet space.
Place your hands on your heart, belly, or anywhere that feels grounding.
Set a timer.

Then speak — out loud if possible, gently if not.

- *"I am enough."*
- *"I am safe to be myself."*
- *"I am allowed to rest."*
- *"I am worthy of respect and tenderness."*
- *"I trust my body. I trust my knowing. I trust my timing."*
- *"I do not need to earn my place in the world — I already belong."*

It may feel awkward.
Your mind might resist.
Your critic might whisper: *"You're just saying words."*

But keep going.
Because the repetition is the healing.
The body doesn't know the difference between what is real and what is imagined.
So the more you tell it something new — something loving — the more it begins to believe.

Here's what happens when you do this consistently:

- Your nervous system softens.
- Your reactions slow down.
- Your decisions become clearer.
- Your emotional spirals become shorter.
- Your tolerance for mistreatment disappears.
- Your connection to joy increases.
- Your sense of being anchored in yourself deepens.

This isn't magic. It's maintenance. And just like physical fitness, emotional and energetic fitness builds through small, repeated action.

Five minutes a day can change how you live in your own body.
Five minutes a day can become the difference between spiralling and self-holding.
Five minutes a day can become the foundation of a lifetime of peace.

Understanding Women

Radical Acceptance of Your Own Humanity

You are not here to be perfect.
You are here to be whole.

And wholeness includes all of it:

- The parts you're proud of.
- The parts you hide.
- The parts you haven't figured out yet.
- The parts you swore you'd healed until they came back again.

Radical self-love begins where perfection ends.
It's not about becoming the most evolved version of yourself.
It's about learning how to hold yourself through your most human moments without shame.

Self-love means letting yourself be a work in progress — without self-punishment.

Some days you will regress.
Some days you will react.
Some days you'll catch yourself in old habits, old thoughts, old stories.
And that's not failure.

That's feedback.
It's your system asking: "Can we do *it differently this time?*"

But most women don't answer that question with compassion.
They answer it with self-attack.

- *"I should know better."*
- *"Why am I still like this?"*
- *"No one else is struggling this much."*

Understanding Women

Except they are.
They just don't say it out loud.

You don't need to be exceptional. You need to be honest.

Your worth isn't conditional. It doesn't come from how calm you are, how graceful you are, or how much you've "healed." It comes from being here, exactly as you are, and choosing to meet yourself with kindness — even when it's hard.

This is what radical self-love looks like:

- Naming your shame and still showing up.
- Owning your flaws without making them your identity.
- Apologising without collapsing.
- Celebrating yourself without guilt.
- Being messy and magnificent, sometimes in the same breath.

This isn't permission to avoid growth.
It's the foundation that makes growth sustainable.
Because no one thrives under the weight of constant self-rejection.

You are not here to become flawless. You are here to become real.

And real is full of layers.
Full of contradictions.
Full of power that can only be accessed when you stop trying to "fix" yourself and start allowing yourself to be yourself.

That's what makes you magnetic.
That's what makes you safe to love.
That's what makes your presence healing — not just to others, but to you.

Radical acceptance isn't about giving up.
It's about finally coming home.

Understanding Women

Letting Self-Love Lead the Way in All Decisions

Most people make decisions from fear.

Fear of not being liked.
Fear of missing out.
Fear of losing approval, attention, love.
Fear of being seen as selfish, difficult, or too much.

And so they say yes when their body says no.
They stay quiet when their soul wants to speak.
They shape-shift, overgive, overwork, over-explain — then wonder why they feel resentful, anxious, or disconnected.

But when self-love leads, the choices become clear.

Self-love says: I am allowed to honour what's right for me.

Not because it's comfortable.
Not because it's easy.
But because it's aligned.

When self-love leads, you stop choosing from guilt, obligation, or people-pleasing.
You stop sacrificing your peace for other people's comfort.
You stop asking, "*What will they think of me?*" and start asking, "*What do I want to think of myself?*"

You choose:

- Rest over proving.
- Honesty over harmony.
- Boundaries over burnout.
- Your own inner knowing over anyone else's projection.

Understanding Women

And suddenly, the world feels less chaotic — not because it changed, but because you stopped betraying yourself inside it.

Letting self-love lead is a compass, not a costume.

It's not about "acting" confident.
It's about *being* centred.
It's not about looking healed.
It's about living in integrity.

This kind of leadership begins quietly.
It begins with tiny choices, every day, that say:

- *"I choose me."*
- *"I can love myself through this."*
- *"I trust myself to handle the outcome of being honest."*
- *"I am worthy of the life I want — and I'm willing to live in alignment with it."*

That is not selfish.
That is self-responsible.
And that is what makes your presence powerful.

When self-love leads, life doesn't get easier — it gets cleaner.

Cleaner boundaries.
Cleaner choices.
Cleaner communication.
Cleaner energy.

You still face fear, but you don't make decisions from it.
You still feel doubt, but you don't shrink for it.
You still make mistakes, but you don't weaponise them against your worth.

Self-love becomes the voice inside you that says: "No matter what happens — *I will not abandon myself again.*" And from that place, everything changes.

Understanding Women

Chapter 20: Financial Freedom and Female Creation

"Financial freedom isn't about chasing worth. It's about remembering you were valuable long before anyone could price it. When you stop asking for permission to be valuable, you start building the life your soul always knew was yours."

— ***Heather***

The Energetics of Earning – and Why Women Hesitate

Money is not just currency.
It is an energy swap.
It is expression.
It is the physical manifestation of value, exchange, and belief.

And for many women, it is loaded with hesitation.

Not because women don't want financial freedom — but because, deep down, many have been taught they don't deserve it. Or that claiming it will cost them love, safety, or belonging. The feminine relationship with earning is different.

Masculine energy tends to pursue earning as a direct, linear goal:
"I want this. I go after it. I achieve."

Feminine energy doesn't move in a straight line.
It flows.
It creates.
It aligns.

It wants to feel good in the doing, not just validated by the result.

Understanding Women

But the world of money has not been built for flow.
It has been built for pressure. Performance. Proof.

So what happens?

Women force themselves into masculine structures of achievement — and burn out.
Or they stay in flow without structure — and can't sustain.

Neither extreme works.

At the root of it all is this: worth.

When a woman hesitates to earn, she's rarely just afraid of money.
She's afraid of what receiving that much value might say about her.

- *"Will people think I'm greedy?"*
- *"Will I be judged for charging too much?"*
- *"Will my family still relate to me if I earn more than them?"*
- *"Will I be safe if I'm fully financially independent?"*

Underneath most money blocks isn't laziness or lack of ambition.
It's fear of separation.
Fear of judgment.
Fear of becoming "too much" to be loved.

So women shrink. They play small. They ask for less.

They wait to be chosen instead of creating their own seat at the table.
They discount their work.
They downplay their impact.
They talk about helping others — but don't allow themselves to receive abundance in return.

And then they resent the systems, the people, the structures — but continue participating in them.

This is the energetic loop that must be broken.

Because earning is not about hustle.
It is about alignment.

When a woman aligns her self-worth with her creative expression, and channels that into something tangible — she becomes magnetic.

Not because she's trying to prove anything.
But because her energy says: "*This is valuable. And so am I.*"

Building Relationship with Money as a Mirror of Self-Worth

Money isn't just a practical tool.
It's a mirror.
It reflects your beliefs, boundaries, and self-concept in real time.

Most people think money is about math.
But it's actually about identity.

Because how you relate to money is how you relate to yourself.

Do you trust yourself to receive?

Do you feel guilt when money comes in?
Do you apologise when you state your prices?
Do you overgive in exchange for underpayment?
Do you hesitate before investing in yourself?

That's not about cash flow.
That's about worthiness.

Women have been trained to associate money with discomfort:

- *"Good girls don't ask for more."*

Understanding Women

- *"It's greedy to want financial freedom."*
- *"Who does she think she is to charge that?"*
- *"Money will make me less spiritual, less grounded, less kind."*

None of these are truths.
They are inherited beliefs.

And as long as those beliefs go unchallenged, you'll keep trying to create abundance while still questioning whether you're allowed to receive it. You cannot receive more than you believe you're allowed to hold.

Money doesn't respond to hustle. It responds to energetic congruence.

If you say, "I want to earn more," but you undercharge, undervalue, overdeliver, or apologise for your offerings — you are sending mixed signals to your field.

Energetically, you are leaking. The moment you clean up those leaks — money begins to respond differently.

Not just because of strategy.
But because your inner world has shifted into coherence.

This is not about worshipping money. It's about making peace with it.

Money is not evil.
It is not spiritual or unspiritual.
It's a neutral force that simply expands the energy of the person holding it.

If you are generous, loving, grounded — money will magnify that.
If you are fearful, controlling, reactive — money will magnify that too.

So the question is not: *"How do I earn more?"* It's: *"Who am I becoming with what I already have?"*

Because the energy of earning begins within.
And money will always meet you where your self-worth already lives.

Understanding Women

Creating from the Feminine — Flow, Beauty, and Purpose

Women don't just want to make money.
They want to make meaning.

They want to create from beauty, from truth, from soul.
They want to feel *alive* in their work — not drained by it.
They want what they build to have resonance, not just revenue.

This is the path of feminine creation.

And it's not a weaker path.
It's a wiser one.

Feminine creation begins in the body.

It starts with presence.
With noticing what feels good, what feels aligned, what lights you up.
It's intuitive, not linear.
Sensory, not strategic.

It doesn't ask, "*What will sell?*"
It asks, "*What wants to move through me?*"

It doesn't chase outcomes.
It magnetises opportunity through coherence.

It is deeply *in service* — but never in sacrifice.

And when a woman creates from this place, what she offers carries frequency.
It lands in people's fields in a way they can feel.
Because it was made from a place of alignment, not performance.

But this kind of creation requires permission.

Permission to:

Understanding Women

- Let go of how it's "supposed" to look.
- Create something even if no one claps for it.
- Trust beauty as a form of intelligence.
- Build slow, seasonal, sustainable growth.
- Redefine success in your own words.
- Honour rest as a critical part of the creative cycle.

Feminine creation is cyclical.
It spirals.
It deepens.
It does not force itself open before it's ready.

If your creations don't match what the world praises — but they feel true to you — that's still success.

Because you are not here to build what already exists.
You are here to channel something only *you* can bring through.

Purpose is not something you chase. It's something you *become*.

You become it by following the breadcrumbs of joy.
By trusting the subtle pull.
By letting the process of building feel just as meaningful as the result.

Feminine creation is an act of devotion.
Not to productivity.
But to *truth*.

When you create from this place, the money comes. Not because you chased it — but because your energy was aligned enough to *receive it*.

Understanding Women

When to Walk Away and Build Your Own Empire

There comes a moment in every woman's journey where she realises she can no longer fit herself into systems that were never built for her soul.

The workplace that demands her masculine energy 24/7.
The relationship that thrives on her shrinking.
The business model that rewards burnout over brilliance.

She can patch it.
She can negotiate with it.
She can try to soften the sharp edges.

But eventually, the truth gets too loud to ignore: It's not her that's broken. It's the container. And the only thing left to do is walk away.

Walking away is not weakness. It's wisdom.

It's the wisdom to know:

- *"I am no longer available for my own diminishment."*
- *"I am not here to fight for scraps of validation."*
- *"I am not going to keep exhausting myself to prove a worth that was never in question."*

It is not about quitting. It's about choosing.

Choosing to build a life, a business, a body of work, a relationship, a way of living — that honours your whole self.
Choosing to create your own empire, even if it starts as a single brick.
Choosing to trust your own timing, even when the world demands urgency.
Choosing to believe that flow, beauty, creativity, compassion, and peace are not luxuries for later. They are necessities for now.

Building your own empire doesn't mean doing it alone.

Understanding Women

It means:

- Choosing collaborators who celebrate your boundaries, not resent them.
- Choosing clients, customers, partners, and friends who resonate with your truth.
- Choosing to move in spaces where your energy expands — not contracts.

Your empire might be a company. It might be a practice. It might be a garden, a family, a body of art, a way of being.

It doesn't have to look big from the outside. It has to feel sovereign on the inside.

Because here's the truth:

You were never meant to beg for space at tables that require you to leave parts of yourself at the door.

You were meant to build your own table.
Your own field.
Your own world.

And when you do — you don't just free yourself. You become the lighthouse that shows every woman still stuck inside a broken system that there is another way.

Not through fighting.
Not through proving.

Through being.

Through embodying what it looks like to live fully, freely, and fiercely as yourself.

This is what feminine creation leads to:
Not just surviving.
But building worlds worth living in.

Chapter 21: A World Worth Belonging To

"When the world no longer feels safe to be feminine or masculine, neutrality becomes the refuge. But safety isn't found in erasing identity — it's found in healing the energy beneath"

— **Heather**

Why Gender Neutrality Is a Response to Energetic Suffering

When the world no longer feels safe to be feminine — and no longer feels safe to be masculine — what's left?

Neutrality.

Not because neutrality is inherently wrong.
But because it has become a survival response to deep, unhealed energetic suffering.

We have spent generations misunderstanding the energies inside us:

- Masculine energy: distorted into domination, control, suppression.
- Feminine energy: distorted into submission, weakness, invisibility.

When masculine energy became aggressive instead of protective — when feminine energy became self-abandoning instead of self-honouring — the human system broke down.

It became safer to be neither.
Or to oscillate between the two in ways that didn't feel real, embodied, or natural.

Understanding Women

Because being firmly rooted in either energy had become dangerous.
Being masculine could mean being violent, cold, unreachable, detached.
Being feminine could mean being diminished, controlled, unsafe, passive aggressive.

So instead, the collective energy began to move toward erasing the distinction altogether.

Not because gender itself was the problem — but because the distortions of those energies made identity feel like a threat.

Gender neutrality is not the enemy. It's the symptom.

It's the symptom of a world that failed to nurture both energies with dignity.
It's the symptom of a system that turned protection into power abuse and nurturing into sacrifice.

When the energetic foundations are broken, the structures built on them can no longer hold.

And so we see it now:

- The rejection of traditional roles — not because roles are wrong, but because the energies within them became distorted.
- The blurring of identity — not because humans are confused, but because they are traumatised.
- The struggle to belong anywhere — not because the world has changed beyond hope, but because the soul can no longer breathe inside old systems.

This isn't about going backwards. It's about remembering what was true before it was twisted.

Masculine energy at its healthiest is protective, holding, honouring.
Feminine energy at its healthiest is creative, nurturing, expansive.

Neither energy is superior.
Neither energy is secondary.

Neither energy is aggressive.
Both are sacred.
Both are necessary.

And *both* have been *deeply* wounded.

The healing we need now isn't about forcing people back into rigid roles.

It's about healing the energetic distortions so that however a person expresses themselves — whether traditionally, fluidly, or uniquely — they are doing so from a place of wholeness, not wounding.

Making Masculine and Feminine Feel Safe Again

We cannot heal the world without healing the energies that move through it.
And we cannot heal those energies if we only point fingers outward.

The masculine has been distorted, yes.
But so has the feminine.

Aggression is not the sole domain of men.
Women, too, have weaponised their wounds.

Emotional aggression — the sharpness, the judgment, the gossip, the withdrawal of love as punishment, the need to be right at any cost — is as damaging to the energetic fabric of humanity as physical aggression.

It erodes trust.
It fractures connection.
It seeds fear in the very spaces where safety is meant to be cultivated.

And the consequences are not invisible.

Emotional aggression leaves scars.

It:

- Damages nervous systems.
- Increases anxiety, isolation, and emotional shutdown.
- Blocks intuition.
- Corrodes self-worth.
- Fractures the ability to experience deep, nourishing love.
- Ripples outward into communities, families, relationships, and systems.

Every time a woman attacks another woman — every time a woman attacks herself — every time a woman uses emotional dominance instead of emotional responsibility — she adds to the collective suffering that she herself longs to be free from.

And it's important to understand:

You cannot think two thoughts at the same time.
You cannot hold judgment and peace in the same breath.
You cannot attack yourself or others without attacking the energy of the world itself.

This isn't to create shame.
It's to create awakening.

Because when women truly understand the power of their emotional energy, they stop using it as a weapon — and start using it as a force for healing.

Healing is not about controlling behaviour. It's about changing energy.

You can force yourself to "be nice."
You can censor your words.
You can perform kindness.

But if underneath it you are seething, judging, resenting — your energy will still carry violence.
And the body — yours and others' — will feel it.

Understanding Women

The only way to truly heal is to transform the energy at its root.
And that begins with making both masculine and feminine energies feel safe again.

- The masculine must feel safe to hold without being accused of controlling.
- The feminine must feel safe to flow without being accused of weakness.
- Strength must be redefined as presence, not dominance.
- Compassion must be redefined as clarity, not martyrdom

When aggression drops, space opens.
When judgment softens, connection grows.
When emotional literacy replaces emotional weaponry, peace becomes possible — not just internally, but globally.

You are not responsible for the whole world's healing. But you are responsible for your energy in it.

Every choice you make to soften your judgment — every moment you choose curiosity over criticism — every time you stay present instead of projecting — you are repairing the energetic web of life.

You are making it safer for all beings — masculine, feminine, or fluid — to exist.

You are becoming the peace you say you long for.

It doesn't happen out there first.
It happens in here — inside your own field.

And that is how the world begins to heal:
One woman, one choice, one energetic shift at a time.

Understanding Women

Living as a Compassionate Woman with Clear Boundaries

Compassion without boundaries is self-destruction.
Boundaries without compassion are walls.

The new womanhood we are building needs both.

Not as opposites — but as partners in strength.

Compassion is not martyrdom.

It's not sacrificing your truth to keep others comfortable.
It's not shrinking to avoid someone else's insecurities.
It's not tolerating mistreatment in the name of "being kind."

Real compassion is clear.
It is grounded in reality.
It honours both your humanity and theirs.

It says:

- *"I see your pain — but I won't let it bleed all over my life."*
- *"I understand your struggle — but I am not responsible for your healing."*
- *"I can hold empathy for you — and still hold the line that protects my peace."*

Boundaries are an act of compassion — first for yourself, then for others.

Because when you have no boundaries, you breed resentment.
You start blaming others for what you allowed.
You start leaking energy and calling it "giving."
You lose the clarity and calm that make your presence safe, magnetic, healing.

Boundaries aren't walls to keep people out. They are the structures that allow love, creativity, and connection to thrive without fear of invasion.

Understanding Women

Without boundaries, compassion turns into self-betrayal.
Without compassion, boundaries turn into control.

The feminine thrives when both are alive inside her:
Soft heart.
Strong spine.

A compassionate woman with clear boundaries is a force.

She doesn't manipulate.
She doesn't martyr.
She doesn't control.
She doesn't need to be rescued.

She leads herself.
She loves from fullness, not from emptiness.
She connects deeply — but she knows where she ends, and others begin.

And because of that — her love is real.
Her energy is clean.
Her impact is lasting.

This is the foundation of the world worth belonging to:

- Women who stay open, without staying naïve.
- Women who stay soft, without sacrificing their truth.
- Women who love themselves enough to say, "*I* choose peace, not performance."

The future isn't built by women who collapse under pressure or harden into resentment.
It's built by women who know how to hold their compassion and their boundaries in the same breath.

And every time you choose that — you are laying another brick in the foundation of the world we are all trying to return to.

Understanding Women

Becoming the Feminine Role Model You Always Needed

You may not have had the role models you deserved growing up.

Maybe you had a mother who sacrificed herself until there was nothing left.
Maybe you had a sister who competed instead of supported.
Maybe you had teachers who praised compliance but not creativity.
Maybe you had friends who gossiped, judged, or abandoned when you grew.

You were shown distorted versions of feminine energy, and somewhere inside you learned:

- *"It's safer not to shine."*
- *"It's better to belong by shrinking."*
- *"If I'm soft, I'll be hurt."*
- *"If I'm strong, I'll be punished."*

But here's the truth:

You are not here to repeat the patterns you inherited.
You are here to become the pattern breaker.

The woman you needed back then? You are building her now.

She is not flawless.
She is not endlessly patient, endlessly giving, endlessly available.

She is real.

She owns her boundaries.
She speaks her truth.
She stands in her feminine energy without apology or performance.
She loves — but she does not lose herself in love.
She nurtures — but she does not martyr herself for others.

Understanding Women

She shows that kindness and strength are not opposites.
She shows that tenderness is not weakness.
She shows that beauty, creativity, and intuition are not luxuries — they are necessities.

You don't need to save the whole world. You just need to embody the energy you wish the world had more of.

Every time you:

- Choose compassion over control,
- Choose truth over performance,
- Choose presence over projection,
- Choose healing over blaming,

... you are becoming the woman you once needed.

And you are showing the next generation — your daughters, your nieces, your students, your community — that another way is possible.

You are showing them that feminine energy can be powerful, grounded, safe, loving, and clear.
You are showing them that it's safe to be fully themselves.

This isn't about pressure. It's about power.

You don't have to be perfect to lead.
You just have to be willing to live aligned.

Your life becomes your teaching.
Your energy becomes your influence.
Your presence becomes the lighthouse.

You become the woman who didn't just wish the world would change.
You become the woman who quietly, fiercely, lovingly — was the change.

And in doing so, you make the world a place worth belonging to again.

Part Eight: The Return of True Feminine Energy

Understanding Women

Chapter 22: Self-Love as Sacred Practice

"Most of what we call love is control in disguise. Real love doesn't cling, collapse, or perform. It expands you. You can't feel love until you stop performing it. You can't receive love until you stop chasing it. You can't live love until you start becoming it."

— **Heather**

What Is Love — Emotional, Energetic, and Conditional

Love is not just a feeling.
It's a frequency.
It's an energy.
And it's one of the most misunderstood forces on the planet.

We talk about love like it's an emotion we fall into. But most of what we call "love" is actually a combination of conditioning, projection, familiarity, and hope.

We're taught to seek love.
To earn it.
To prove we deserve it.
To mistake attachment, admiration, approval, or relief for the real thing.

And so love becomes confusing, heavy, and conditional.

Conditional love says: "*I love you when...*"

- "When you behave the way I want."
- "When you meet my needs before your own."
- "When you never change."
- "When you make me feel a certain way."

Understanding Women

It might feel like love.
But it's rooted in control.

It says, "*I will love you as long as you don't trigger my wounds.*" Or "*I will love you as long as you play your part in the story I've written in my mind.*"

This is not the love our hearts long for.
This is the version most of us were taught.

And because of that — we become afraid of real love.

Real love is different. Energetically, it's expansive.

Love, in its highest form, doesn't cling or control.
It doesn't demand or diminish.
It allows.

It includes boundaries.
It includes space.
It includes truth.

Energetically, real love is a clean current.
It flows between two people without hooks, expectations, or the need to be right.

Emotionally, it feels like safety and aliveness at the same time.
It says: "*You don't have to be perfect. You just have to be real.*"

But here's the catch: You cannot experience real love *if you don't know how to feel.*

And most people — especially women — were never taught to feel clearly.
We were taught to think our feelings.
To perform our emotions.
To turn love into a job description.

So we chase love.
Or we repel it.
Or we settle for proximity and call it connection.

All while wondering why it still doesn't feel quite right.

Love cannot be fully felt until it is energetically understood.

Not just intellectually.
Not just romantically.
But energetically. Emotionally. Honestly.

Love is a state of being before it's a transaction.
It lives in your nervous system, not your Instagram posts.
It's felt in the spaces where you stop performing and start allowing.

To return to love, we have to return to *feeling*.
To softness.
To honesty.
To a deeper emotional literacy that lets love be clean — without agenda.

Why Feeling Our Feelings Is Essential to Feeling Love

Love is a feeling.
And yet, so many people try to experience it without ever truly *feeling* at all.

We talk about love.
We think about love.
We analyse whether we are in love, or out of love, or falling into it, or losing it.

But we rarely drop into the one place love actually lives: the emotional body.

You can't feel love if you can't feel, full stop.

If you suppress your sadness — you dull your ability to feel joy.
If you deny your anger — you narrow your capacity to feel passion.
If you numb your fear — you close down the vulnerability that love needs in order to land.

Emotional avoidance and emotional connection cannot exist in the same breath.
You cannot block one feeling and still expect to experience another in its fullness.

Understanding Women

Love is not selective. It flows through an open system. And if the system is shut down, love cannot be felt in its true form — no matter how present it may be.

Most women don't realise how emotionally disconnected they are.

They say "I'm in love" — but it's often attachment, familiarity, or fantasy.
They say "I feel unloved" — but it's often that they've stopped being emotionally available to themselves.
They say "I want to be loved for who I am" — but they haven't yet loved *themselves* for who they are.

This isn't a flaw. It's the result of generations of conditioning that taught women to perform emotions, not process them. To think feelings instead of feel them. To speak about love without ever allowing it to move through the body.

Feeling is how we return to love.

Not performance.
Not proof.
Not pleasing.

Just feeling.

- Feeling the grief that you've never been fully seen.
- Feeling the shame of believing you had to earn love.
- Feeling the fear of being rejected when you stop performing.
- Feeling the soft ache of finally letting your guard down.
- Feeling the beauty of being met, held, honoured.

Love doesn't happen in the mind.
It doesn't happen through control.
It happens when the walls come down.
When the emotional system softens.
When you stop trying to win love, and start *letting it in*.

Understanding Women

The Confusion Between Thinking Love and Feeling Love

You can't think your way into love.
You can only feel your way into it.

And yet — so many women are trying to "figure out" love with their minds:

- *"Does he really love me?"*
- *"Is this the right person?"*
- *"Am I still in love?"*
- *"Why does this not feel like it used to?"*

These questions sound emotional.
But most of the time, they're intellectual cover-ups for emotional avoidance.

Because when you're disconnected from your feelings, your mind takes over.
It tries to analyse, dissect, explain, and solve... instead of simply feeling what's true.

Thinking love leads to stories. Feeling love leads to truth.

Thinking love looks like:

- Trying to control how the other person shows up.
- Overanalysing every text, word, or gesture.
- Saying someone is a "good catch" when deep inside, there is unease.
- Needing constant reassurance.
- Comparing what you have to someone else's highlight reel.
- Obsessing over what "should" be happening.

Feeling love looks like:

- Letting your body register what's real.
- Knowing when something feels clean, safe, open, or expansive.
- Being able to feel your own nervous system settle in someone's presence.
- Not needing to "discuss" a relationship because your inner knowing is enough.

Understanding Women

- Being honest about your needs — without apology.
- Recognising what your emotional system is telling you — even when it's not what your ego wants to hear.

The mind makes love conditional.
The body tells the truth about whether love is truly present.

You don't fall out of love. You fall out of emotional connection.

So many women say:

- *"I just don't feel anything anymore."*
- *"Something's missing."*
- *"He's doing everything right, but it's not landing."*

The reason often isn't the other person.
It's that you've stopped feeling love in your body.

Maybe because you've gone into survival mode.
Maybe because your nervous system doesn't feel safe.
Maybe because love has always been a transaction for you, and now the terms have changed.
Maybe because your heart was never fully in it — you just thought it was.

Love has to be felt to be real. Not explained. Not performed. Not maintained through effort. And to feel love, you have to be willing to feel.

To soften.
To risk being vulnerable.
To let the body tell you whether something is love — or whether it's just familiar, or safe, or flattering.

You cannot know love until you stop intellectualising it.

You cannot live love until you feel it moving through your whole system — not just your head.

Understanding Women

The Feminine Heart as a Channel for Love, Not a Vessel of Pain

The feminine heart is not a container for suffering.
It's a conduit for truth.

But somewhere along the way, we were taught that being loving meant being long-suffering.

We were taught that to be a "good woman" meant:

- To absorb other people's pain.
- To carry the emotional weight of relationships.
- To hold it together when others fall apart.
- To stay silent to keep the peace.
- To turn the other cheek, even when our soul is breaking.

And so our hearts became heavy.
Not with love — but with burden.

But a healthy heart doesn't store pain. It lets it move.

Your heart was never meant to hold it all.
It was meant to feel, to process, to release.

The feminine heart in its true essence is:

- Open, not porous.
- Strong, not hardened.
- Wise, not self-sacrificing.
- Compassionate, not collapsing.
- Receptive, not leaking.

You are not here to carry the pain of others in place of love.
You are here to be a channel — to let love *move through* you, not get stuck *inside* you.

Understanding Women

You are not a container for other people's unprocessed emotions.

If someone loves you, they will not make you responsible for carrying what they refuse to face.
And if you love someone, you will not make your value dependent on how much of their pain you can absorb.

This is the distortion the feminine has carried for centuries:

- That love means carrying.
- That presence means absorbing.
- That connection means self-erasure.

But the true feminine heart says: "*I love deeply — but I do not carry what is not mine.*"

Love doesn't ask you to break yourself. It asks you to be yourself.

When the feminine heart is whole and nourished, it becomes a source of light. Not because it is unbreakable — but because it is fluid, true, and connected to something deeper than ego.

That's what makes it a channel.

A woman who is in love with herself — who can feel deeply without drowning, open without leaking, and connect without collapsing — becomes a presence of peace and power.

She doesn't just give love.
She is love.
Not because she tries — but because she allows.

Understanding Women

Chapter 23: The Return of Intuition, Sensitivity, and Creative Power

"You are not here to chase, to prove, or to harden. You are here to create, to feel, to trust, and to return to the river of truth running through your own being."

— **Heather**

Reclaiming Emotion as Intelligence and Sensitivity as Strength

You were never too sensitive.
You were never too emotional.
You were just surrounded by a world that didn't know how to value what you felt.

And so, like many women, you learned to doubt your own depth.
You learned to hide your softness, to dismiss your tears, to label your intuition as irrational.
You learned that logic was rewarded, while sensitivity was punished.
And you learned to betray your feelings in exchange for belonging.

But let's be clear:
Emotion is intelligence.
Sensitivity is strength.

And reclaiming them is not weakness. It's your return to wholeness.

Emotion is not chaos. It's data.

Emotion is the body's way of signalling what's true.

- Anger tells you where your boundaries were crossed.

- Grief tells you what mattered.
- Anxiety tells you where your nervous system feels unsafe.
- Joy tells you what aligns with your soul.
- Peace tells you when you're home in yourself.

Your emotional system is a finely tuned guidance mechanism.
It is not here to be silenced.
It's here to be listened to, respected, and used as a compass.

The more fluent you become in your emotional language, the more you realise how intelligent your feelings have always been.

Sensitivity is not a flaw. It's a gift.

To be sensitive is to be attuned.
It's to notice what others miss.
It's to pick up on energy shifts, unspoken words, subtle changes in tone, vibration, intention.

It's to feel into a room, into a person, into a moment — and know what's really going on beneath the surface.

But in a world addicted to speed, force, and disconnection, sensitivity gets labelled as fragile.

It's not.

It's a superpower.

Sensitivity is not about being overwhelmed.
It's about being open.
And when you learn how to work with it — ground it, understand it, honour it — you stop collapsing under it and start channelling through it.

You were not made to be numb. You were made to feel.

That's where your power lives.

Not in the numbing.
Not in the bypassing.
Not in the over-functioning and emotional self-erasure.

Your feminine essence flows through feeling.
Through your ability to receive, to intuit, to know what's happening without being told.
Through your capacity to hold emotion without drowning in it.

And the more you reclaim your emotion and sensitivity as strengths, the more you become who you were always meant to be.

Not hardened.
Not collapsed.
But fully alive in your intelligence — emotional, energetic, and intuitive.

Awakening Intuition as the Inner Authority

There is a voice inside you that has always known.

It doesn't shout.
It doesn't compete.
It doesn't rush.

But it is there — waiting — beneath the noise of logic, fear, overthinking, and performance.

That voice is your intuition.
And it is your truest inner authority.

You don't have to go outside yourself for every answer.

You don't need endless feedback, second opinions, or signs.
You don't need permission to know what you already feel is true.

Understanding Women

Intuition is not about magic.
It's not about being "special."
It's not even about certainty.

It's about honesty.
It's about listening to the part of you that doesn't explain, it just *knows*.

Intuition is ancient. It's intelligent. And it's always been with you.

The problem is not that your intuition doesn't work.
It's that you've been trained to override it.

You were praised for being agreeable — not perceptive.
You were taught to prioritise others' needs, logic, and authority over your own knowing.
You were taught to justify your choices, defend your insights, and make sense to other people — before trusting yourself.

And in doing so, your intuition got quieter.
Not because it left.
But because your nervous system didn't feel safe enough to follow it.

Intuition awakens when the body feels safe.

When you start:

- Calming your system,
- Listening without doubting,
- Acting on what you know instead of explaining it away —

... your intuition strengthens.

It becomes your compass.
Your centre.
Your clarity in the fog.

And you stop looking outward for every answer — because you know you already carry what you need.

This is what it means to trust yourself.

Not because you have every answer.
But because you know how to listen to the voice that's never stopped speaking.

It doesn't come from your head.
It doesn't come from other people.
It comes from you — your soul, your energy, your body's subtle language.

And once that voice becomes louder than the fear — you begin to live aligned with something far more intelligent than logic.

You begin to live as a woman who trusts herself.

The Shift from Chasing to Attracting Through Feminine Magnetism

You were not born to chase.
You were born to attract.

But if you've spent most of your life chasing — approval, success, love, attention, worth — it's not your fault. It's conditioning.

You were taught that if you didn't chase it, you'd never have it.
That if you didn't prove yourself, you wouldn't be chosen.
That if you weren't loud, loud enough, or loud in the right way — you'd be overlooked, underestimated, or forgotten.

So you ran and then tried to manipulate.
After love.
After opportunity.
After people who were never meant to be caught.

Understanding Women

But feminine power doesn't chase nor seek to control. It magnetises and allows to flow freely.

The more you step into your own energy — clear, grounded, sovereign, full — the more what's meant for you comes forward.

Because magnetism is not magic.
It's *energetic congruence.*

When your inner world aligns with your essence, your truth, your peace — you stop trying to manipulate outcomes.
You stop exhausting yourself in pursuit.
You start letting life meet you where you are — not where you *perform to be.*

Attracting doesn't mean doing nothing. It means doing the right things for the right reasons.

You don't stop taking action.
You stop taking *disempowered* action.

You stop chasing love that isn't reciprocated.
You stop justifying yourself to people who aren't even listening.
You stop proving your value to people who can't see it because they don't yet see their own.

And instead, you become magnetic through:

- Peace.
- Purpose.
- Pleasure.
- Presence.

Not because you're trying to impress, but because you are radiating what is true.

The feminine doesn't force. She flows.

And when she flows from inner safety, from grounded power, from emotional intelligence, from self-trust — she becomes a beacon.

Not to get attention.
But to attract resonance.

She no longer needs to chase what doesn't see her.
She waits in wholeness for what is aligned to recognise her.

And it does.

Because energy doesn't lie.

The Creatrix, the Healer, and the Sacred Flow of Feminine Energy

You are not just a woman.
You are a force.
A channel.
A vessel for life-force, wisdom, restoration, and creation.

When you stop trying to survive the world that wounded your softness, you begin to remember who you are beneath it all.

You are the Creatrix — the one who births not only children, but visions, ideas, environments, and energy.
You are the Healer — not because you fix others, but because your presence becomes a space where others can meet themselves more honestly.
And you are the Flow — not the chaos or the storm, but the still, deep river of knowing that runs beneath all performance, fear, and control.

You are not too much. You are exactly enough.

You were never meant to be linear, logical, always-on, always-in-control.

Understanding Women

You were made to:

- Create in waves.
- Feel in seasons.
- Move in cycles.
- Expand and contract with life itself.

This is not a flaw. It is a sacred rhythm.
And when you honour that rhythm — your intuition strengthens, your energy clears, your nervous system calms, and your power returns.

True feminine energy doesn't dominate. It doesn't demand.

It creates.

- It creates safety through presence.
- It creates beauty through intention.
- It creates growth through nourishment, not pressure.
- It creates change not by fighting — but by holding an unwavering field of truth and love.

This is the sacred feminine flow.
This is not the version you've seen distorted by performance or diluted by pop spirituality.
This is the original pulse of creative life-force that lives inside you.

And when you return to this space — you don't just feel better.
You become magnetic, grounded, radiant, whole.

You stop seeking healing.
You start living it.

You are not here to be small. You are here to be sovereign.

Understanding Women

The Creatrix doesn't ask for permission.
She doesn't wait to be chosen.
She creates — boldly, gently, in rhythm with her own soul.

The Healer doesn't rescue.
She remembers her own wholeness and holds space for others to find theirs.

The Sacred Feminine doesn't fight for power.
She becomes it, quietly, deeply, with love.

And that's what this return is really about.

You.

Not becoming someone new — but coming home to the part of you that was never lost.

Understanding Women

Chapter 24: Cosmic Belonging and the Feminine Reunion with Nature

"Your rhythm is ancient. Your softness is strength. Your presence is medicine. When you trust your truth and honour your nature, the world becomes safer for everyone."

— ***Heather***

Remembering the Sacred Cycles of Earth, Moon, and Body

You are not separate from nature.
You are made of it.

Your bones carry the minerals of the mountains.
Your blood moves like the tides.
Your breath mirrors the wind.
Your womb reflects the moon.

But somewhere along the path of progress and performance, we stopped remembering that we are nature.

And in forgetting this, we began treating our bodies, our emotions, and our rhythms as problems to be fixed — instead of wisdom to be honoured.

The feminine is cyclical. And so are you.

The Earth does not bloom all year.
The moon does not shine full every night.
The tides rise and fall.
The seasons shift and rest.

Understanding Women

You were not meant to live in constant summer.
You were not made to produce, give, or glow endlessly.
You were made to wax and wane, to root and rise, to bleed and begin again.

But modern life has no room for the sacred pause.
No patience for the quiet season.
No reverence for the inner winter.

So we override. We hustle. We numb.
And then we wonder why we feel disconnected, depleted, lost.

You don't need to return to nature. You need to remember you are part of it.

Your body already knows how to live in harmony.
Your cycle already speaks to the moon.
Your nervous system already listens to the land.

It is your mind that was taught to forget.
Taught to fear rest.
Taught to mistrust your inner knowing.
Taught that consistency means sameness, instead of presence.

But you are not linear.
You are spiral.
You are renewal.
You are sacred pattern and wild potential.

To live in feminine alignment is to honour the rhythm of the Earth, the wisdom of the moon, and the truth of your body.

It's not about being spiritual.
It's about being real.

It's not about performing sacredness.
It's about living it — in breath, in pace, in awareness, in return.

And when you do...

- Your system calms.
- Your intuition strengthens.
- Your energy replenishes.
- Your sense of belonging deepens.

Because the moment you stop pushing against your nature is the moment you come home to it.

Letting Go of Separation and Reuniting with Natural Wisdom

Separation is a lie.

It's the lie that says:

- "*You are alone.*"
- "*You are disconnected.*"
- "*You are too much, or not enough.*"
- "*You are a stranger to the world that birthed you.*"

And it's this illusion of separation — between body and earth, between soul and source, between self and others — that keeps so many women feeling ungrounded, unwell, and unloved.

But separation is not the truth of who you are.
It is the result of forgetting.

You are not separate from nature. You are the expression of it.

Your emotions are as natural as a thunderstorm.
Your softness is as real as spring rain.
Your rage, your joy, your silence, your tears — they all belong to something ancient and wise.

Understanding Women

The only thing unnatural is the belief that you need to earn your place on this planet.

You don't.

You belong by birthright.

You were made of this Earth — her soil, her salt, her breath.

And when you stop trying to dominate, control, suppress, or outperform your natural cycles, you begin to live as you were designed to — in rhythm, in truth, in peace.

Natural wisdom lives inside you. But it only speaks in the present.

It doesn't shout over your busy thoughts.
It doesn't compete with your to-do list.
It doesn't raise its voice when you're rushing, proving, or spinning in self-judgment.

It waits.

It waits for your stillness.
For your breath.
For the moment you choose to drop back into your body and listen.

And when you do, you'll find:

- The answers are already within.
- The signals are already there.
- The reconnection is already happening.

Because wisdom isn't something you find.
It's something you remember.

Understanding Women

You Are Not Too Much — You Are Exactly Right

This world has spent decades trying to shrink women.

Too loud.
Too emotional.
Too sensitive.
Too ambitious.
Too wild.
Too deep.
Too strong.
Too much.

And in response, we've spent years trying to take up less space. We've silenced our truth, dimmed our energy, questioned our joy, and apologised for our presence.

But the truth is:
You were never too much.
You were just *more than this world knew how to hold.*
And that's not a problem with you. That's a signal it's time to live in a different way.

Your too-muchness is not your shame. It is your signal.

It's the part of you that remembers the wild.
The river.
The moonlight.
The sacred breath of the earth.

It's the part of you that still believes in feeling everything, sensing truth in silence, and creating beauty for no reason other than it fills your soul.

That is not weakness.
That is power in its truest form.

But that power only thrives when you stop editing it to be palatable.

Understanding Women

You were not made to be palatable. You were made to be whole.

And wholeness includes:

- Your laughter that comes too loud.
- Your grief that arrives uninvited.
- Your insight that makes others uncomfortable.
- Your body that takes up space.
- Your needs that ask to be met.
- Your energy that doesn't always fit in.

The world has told you to make yourself smaller so you'll be accepted. But the truth is: when you accept yourself fully, you create the world where you already belong.

You don't need to be less.
You need to be aligned.
Fully.
Unapologetically.
Exactly as you are.

Because you are not too much.
You are the medicine you were waiting for.

The Feminine Path Forward: Trust, Flow, and Sacred Living

This is not the end.
This is the return.

The return to yourself.
The return to wisdom that never left.
The return to a way of living that doesn't require you to abandon your softness, harden your heart, or betray your nature just to be seen.

Understanding Women

The future doesn't belong to the loudest voice in the room.
It belongs to the most honest.
The most clear.
The most rooted in what is sacred.

And that begins with you.

The feminine path isn't perfect. It's present.

It's the path of:

- Trusting your body, even when it's tired.
- Trusting your timing, even when the world wants you to rush.
- Trusting your knowing, even when it makes no logical sense.
- Trusting your flow, even when you're surrounded by systems built on force.

It's the path of honouring rhythm over rigidity.
Energy over expectation.
Essence over ego.

And it's a path that doesn't begin with a big moment — it begins with a choice.

The choice to come back to yourself, over and over again.

- When the world tries to make you hustle, you pause.
- When your mind tries to override your feeling, you breathe.
- When your old patterns whisper you're not enough, you soften.
- When the future feels uncertain, you trust your next small step.

This is sacred living.
It's not a performance.
It's not perfection.
It's not a constant high.

Understanding Women

It's a devotion.
To alignment.
To wholeness.
To the living truth of your energy, your soul, your feminine self.

You don't have to change the whole world. You just have to stop betraying yourself.

Because when a woman chooses to live in truth, in rhythm, in trust — the whole frequency of the world shifts.

You are not separate from the healing of this planet.
You are part of it.
You are *essential* to it.

And your softness, your creativity, your boundaries, your joy — they are not indulgent.

They are the medicine of a future where love leads, where peace becomes possible, and where our daughters feel safe in their own skin again.

Conclusion: A Lighthouse, A Mirror, A Map

You didn't need another book telling you how to be better.
You needed a book that helped you remember who you already are.

This was never about becoming something more.
It was about removing everything that never belonged.

Because the truth is — you were always whole.
You were always wise.
You were always powerful.

You just learned to doubt it.

You learned to live in your head instead of your body.
You learned to perform instead of feel.
You learned to carry others instead of letting yourself be held.
You learned to harden instead of honour your softness.
You learned to abandon yourself to be chosen, when the only choice that ever really mattered was your own.

This book is a lighthouse.
To bring you back when the world feels too loud, when the noise of perfection, judgment, shame, and not-enoughness tries to pull you out to sea.

It's a mirror.
To show you where you're still hiding, performing, blaming, or numbing — not so you can feel bad, but so you can get free.

It's a map.
To help you return to the truth of your feminine energy — the kind that creates, nurtures, heals, magnetises, and *feels everything deeply* without apology.

And most of all, it's a love letter.

Understanding Women

To the woman you are now, to the girl you used to be, and to the daughter you have, or might someday raise, whether she walks this earth through your body or through your legacy.

Because every word here has been written with them in mind:
The women who want to feel safe in their own skin.
The women who are ready to stop performing.
The women who are brave enough to look inward, heal what's theirs, and return the rest.

You are not here to shrink.
You are not here to chase.
You are not here to apologise for your rhythm, your feelings, your knowing, or your light.

You are here to be whole.
And from that wholeness — kind.
And from that kindness — powerful.
And from that power — free.

The cage door is open now.

But stepping through it will require a conscious choice.

Choose you.
Choose truth.
Choose to live as if your life belongs to you — because it does.

And let this be your vow: "*I will not abandon myself again. I am coming home.*"

About the Author: Heather Ogilvie

Heather Ogilvie is a global consultant, intuitive guide, energy healer, and the founder of multiple transformative ventures across strategy, healing, business, and soul work. Known for her sharp insight, grounded wisdom, and fierce compassion, she has spent decades helping people reconnect to their truth — whether in the boardroom or the body.

Heather's work bridges emotional intelligence, energetic mastery, and practical strategy. Her signature style is both challenging and kind, calling people into full self-responsibility while offering deep, unwavering support.

She is the author of *The Fast-Track Millionairess*, *The Intelligent Body*, *The Intuitive Body*, and *Understanding Women*, and is the visionary behind the Heather Ogilvie Theory of Life Force Transmission, and a growing body of multidimensional teachings.

Her mission is simple:
To help people remember who they are.
To live with integrity, purpose, and power.
And to create a world where self-worth, softness, strength, and truth are no longer in conflict — but finally in balance.

She lives in Scotland, guided by nature, animals, her spirited essence, and the fierce belief that tenderness is sacred.

Learn more about Heather's work on her website at **www.islaywellness.com**.

Printed in Great Britain
by Amazon